The Secret World of Wombats

JACKIE FRENCH
illustrated by BRUCE WHATLEY

Angus&Robertson
An imprint of HarperCollins*Children's Books*

Angus&Robertson
An imprint of HarperCollins*Children'sBooks*, Australia

First published in Australia in 2005
by HarperCollins*Publishers* Pty Limited
ABN 36 009 913 517
harpercollins.com.au

HarperCollins*Publishers*
Level 13, 201 Elizabeth Street, Sydney, NSW 2000, Australia
Unit D, 63 Apollo Drive, Rosedale, Auckland 0632, New Zealand
A 53, Sector 57, Noida, UP, India
1 London Bridge Street, London SE1 9GF, United Kingdom
2 Bloor Street East, 20th floor, Toronto, Ontario M4W 1A8, Canada
195 Broadway, New York, NY 10007, USA

National Library of Australia Cataloguing-in-publication data:

French, Jackie.
  The secret world of wombats.
  ISBN 978 0 2072 0031 1
  I. Wombats – Juvenile literature. I. Title.
599.24

Cover and internal design by Judi Rowe
Cover and internal illustrations by Bruce Whatley
Typeset in 12 on 17 Esprit Book
Printed and bound in Australia by McPhersons Printing Group

The papers used by HarperCollins in the manufacture of this book are
a natural, recyclable product made from wood grown in sustainable
plantation forests. The fibre source and manufacturing processes meet
recognised international environmental standards, and carry certification.

To Smudge, Fudge, Pudge, Chocolate, Gabby,
Bad Bart, Peanut, Mothball, Golden Dragon, Two-and-a-half,
Pretty Face, Flat White, Big Paws, Grunter, Totally Confused,
Whiskers, Roadbat, even Moriarty ... and all the others.

Thank you for so many years, and a glimpse
into another universe.

THE SECRET WORLD OF WOMBATS was shortlisted for The Wilderness Society's non-fiction book award in the Environment Award for Children's Literature 2006 and for the Patricia Wrightson prize in the 2006 NSW Premier's Literary Awards.

Contents

Introduction

Down under your feet is a secret world. There are underground tunnels, and hidden rooms, and sleeping animals waiting for the night.

It's the world of wombats.

Most people have only seen wombats half asleep in zoos or dead by the side of the road. You won't have seen the secret side of wombats — wombat grins and the wombat games they play. You won't know just how fascinating wombats are, nor such things as:

- Why wombats bite each other's bums!
- How wombats 'talk' to each other with their wombat droppings!
- How baby wombats manage not to go to the toilet in their mother's pouch!
- And how singing is a wonderful way to get really close to a wombat.

I met my first wombat more than thirty years ago. His name was Smudge, and we became friends. In those days I was living mostly by myself in the bush — somehow when you live on your own away from other people it's easier to become close to a wild animal. In many ways I think Smudge was the closest friend I have ever had.

I've lived with many wild wombats since then and I've looked after orphaned baby wombats and studied the way wombats live. Wombats are so very, very different from people. Wombats don't 'see' the world, they smell it. If you say 'bad dog' to a dog it gets embarrassed. Wombats don't do *embarrassed*. If you say 'bad wombat' to a wombat it will ignore you, or bite your ankle.

Sometimes I think knowing wombats is as close as I'll ever come to meeting an alien — wombats are creatures so different from us that it takes decades to understand the way they think and live.

A wombat can be one of the cuddliest animals in the universe once it gets to know you. A baby wombat lives in a pouch, which is like being cuddled twenty-four hours a day. I was sitting beside the vegetable garden early this morning sorting out basil plants and suddenly *whump*! I had a wombat on my lap.

It was Mothball, who we helped to raise from a baby. Now she weighs thirty kilograms, has teeth like a tyrannosaurus and a cloud of dust rises every time you pat her. And she pongs! But how can you not hug a lonely wombat? Besides, if I didn't stop to hug her she'd bite my bum next time I bent down to weed. p.s. Don't try this with a wombat who isn't used to people.

I hope the information in this book helps you to understand the strange and wonderful world of wombats — and to love them too.

Are you a wombat?

Are you covered in fur? No? Then you are definitely not a wombat, unless you are a bald wombat.

Do you have a large, egg-shaped, brown nose? Yes? Then you might be a wombat. (Or a kid who has fallen into the Vegemite jar.)

Do you mostly come out at night? Yes? Then you might be a wombat. (Or a vampire.)

Do you mostly eat grass? (Vampires hardly ever eat grass.)

Do you have tiny eyes, little ears and an even smaller tail? Do you eat roots and sedges and tussocks?

Do you have a pouch, if you're a girl? Have you got long claws and longer whiskers, and do you live in a hole in the ground?

If you've answered yes to all those questions, you are a wombat! (Or else you're a *really* weird kid!)

1

The History
of Wombats

A hundred thousand years ago a giant creature roamed the forests of Australia — places where there are only red sandhills now. It was as big as a furry hippopotamus, nearly three metres long and two metres tall, with flat feet and a broad nose — or maybe a short trunk, like an elephant that's shrunk in the rain.

It was a *Diprotodon opatum*, and I am glad we don't have *Diprotodons* living under our house. (If one small wombat, like Mothball, can bite and claw her way through our back door, I can imagine what a *Diprotodon* would do if it decided it wanted carrots!)

Diprotodon opatum was a close relative of modern wombats. There were many wombat-like animals back in ancient Australia, like *Zygomaturus trilobus* and *Palorchestes azael*. There were also giant kangaroos, massive echidnas and marsupial lions — but a marsupial lion would have had a hard time trying to catch a *Diprotodon opatum*.

Some of these massive beasts — the 'megafauna' — were still alive when humans came to Australia between 50,000 and 60,000 years ago. Some of them were hunted and eaten. Others died as the climate became drier and there wasn't enough grass to feed them. Only their two smaller relatives survived — the wombats with bare noses, *Vombatus*, and those with hairy noses, the *Lasiorhunis* wombats.

The hairy-nosed wombats adapted to the drier world — their descendants still live on the Nullarbor Plain and in the dry grasslands of Queensland. But the bare-nosed wombats retreated to the wet-forest areas of south-east Australia.

Humans and wombats

The Aboriginal people hunted wombats and sometimes ate them. But wombats taste disgusting — they are mostly bone and gristle. And their fur feels like a shaggy doormat. Why bother with wombats when you can hunt kangaroo for meat, or wear silky, soft koala or possum fur?

Wombat fur is coarse and stiff, and was used to make string. Old and baby wombats were sometimes

Diprotodon *wishing that carrots had been invented*

attacked by dingoes, but otherwise wombats were left alone pretty much.

White settlers had been in Australia for ten years before they noticed wombats! This isn't so very strange as wombats are nocturnal animals. They live in their burrows during the day and mostly come out at night — and it's hard to see a brown wombat on a black night unless you have a torch. The early settlers were short of candles and oil for lamps, and nervous of the strange bush sounds around them. They just didn't go out much at night.

How wombats got their name

The first Europeans to discover wombats were sailors shipwrecked on an island in Bass Strait. In 1797 they ate wombats — and every other sort of animal on the island — and when Matthew Flinders rescued them a year later he brought a wombat back to show the governor this weird burrowing 'bear'.

But by then the wombat already had a name — James Wilson, a former convict employed by Governor Hunter, had come across wombats on an expedition to the Blue Mountains. According to him, the local Aboriginal people called it a *whom-batt* — and that's what it's been called ever since.

Dangerous times for wombats

Things changed for wombats when white settlers arrived — cattle and sheep ate the wombats' grass, and the cattle's heavy feet flattened the wombats' burrows. White settlers brought rabbits, too, which ate more grass than the cattle, even in areas where cattle and sheep couldn't reach.

Settlers trapped, poisoned and shot wombats. Farmers still do so in many areas today, even where it is illegal. No fence stops a determined wombat, though you can make wombat gates for them (see Chapter 12). Farmers don't like holes in their fences as their livestock can get through. Some farmers resent any animal that eats the grass which they consider belongs to their sheep and cattle. But a wombat's favourite food is tough native grasses. So wombats actually help to keep in check tough grasses and tussocks and sedges.

Today, southern hairy-nosed wombats live only in a few spots around the Nullarbor Plain, and northern hairy-nosed wombats are nearly extinct, surviving only in one colony in mid-north Queensland.

Bare-nosed wombats — the common wombat — have done a bit better. You'll still find them in most forested land in south-east New South Wales and Victoria and throughout Tasmania.

But the wombat population is going down, mainly because of shooting, trapping, dog attacks, car

hairy-nosed wombat   common wombat

incidents or fierce bushfires (mostly lit by humans) that destroy large areas of bush and national parks, and as a result of competition with sheep and cattle. Most people have no idea how few wombats there are, as they see them grazing by the edge of roads at night where cattle haven't been able to reach the grass. People see dead wombats by the side of the road and think, Hey, there must be lots of wombats about. But in many areas now there are not enough wombats to keep breeding (see Chapter 13).

Wombats live for about fourteen years around our valley, but in other regions they may live for only about five years, especially if it's dry and there isn't much grass. Wombats have lived for more than twenty years in zoos, but in the wild, drought, mange (see Chapter 11), cars and human activities often kill them.

This book is about common wombats. Common wombats are a different species from southern and northern hairy-nosed wombats, but they are all pretty similar in many ways, though the hairy-noses are better adapted for dry areas — they don't need to drink, spend more time underground in the cool, moist shade, and breed in the summer so the baby grows up in the cooler winter.

But common wombats are the ones you'll see most often in the bush or at the zoo. And they are the wombats I live with and have studied.

Who's the greatest — you or a wombat?

- Can you scratch your ear with your (back) feet?
  A wombat can.

- Can you dig with your front feet (hands) while
  pushing dirt out with your back feet? A wombat can.

- Can you chew up tussock and digest it? (Do not
  try this!)

- Can you bite and claw your way through a door to
  get to the carrots? (Do not try this either.)

- Can you leave a hundred droppings a night to
  mark out your territory? (*Definitely* do not try this.
  Or if you do, don't say I told you to.)

2

What is a Wombat?

Wombats live in burrows. They are furry. And the female wombats have a pouch for their baby. Wombats sleep during the day — or are pretty dozy. Even if you see a wombat early in the evening it'll probably be intent on eating. They mostly eat grass or sedges and other young shoots.

A wombat's closest relative is a koala, but wombats are much more intelligent than koalas. The cerebral hemispheres — the brain — of a wombat are proportionately bigger than other marsupials! A koala's cerebral hemispheres are much more poorly developed. A wombat's intelligence is a different sort of intelligence from human beings (see Chapter 8) so few people realise how bright wombats can be.

Wombats are not muddle-headed either. They are the most determined, single-minded animals on earth! Never get between a wombat and its burrow if the

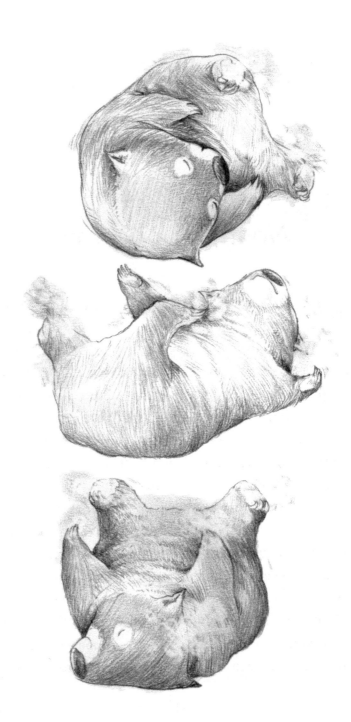

wombat wants to go there — you'll be knocked over!

Wombats *like* dirt. Wombats 'dust bathe' — they wriggle on their backs or tummies in dry dirt or sand. This cleans their fur and helps get rid of ticks and mites. Old wombats especially love dust bathing. They lie on their backs in warm dust, a bit like a person having a nice warm spa bath.

Wombats also *love* freshly dug dirt. Gardening with a wombat is impossible. Every time you plant something the wombat digs it up again. Whenever it rains wombats will be tempted to dig up any nice damp dirt. Mostly they just scratch it a bit, then go back to eating. But wombats think dirt is the most wonderful stuff in the world.

One of the ways a wombat says 'Hi' is to give you a nip. This doesn't hurt other wombats because they have very tough skin. But wombats don't understand why people shriek in agony when their long teeth bite through human flesh.

Bad Bart the biter

Bad Bart bit. He didn't mean to hurt. He was just saying, 'Hello'. If you bent over in the garden Bad Bart would bite your bum. If you sat in a garden chair Bad Bart would bite your ankle.

We had to warn visitors *never* to bend over in the garden, and if a wombat came nosing around the garden table to lift their legs up *high*!

A wombat's body

Wombats are built for burrowing — they are 'dirt machines'. They have tiny eyes, small ears, a short neck and a strong, stocky body, with powerful shoulders and legs.

In fact they look like a brown hairy rock with legs. But they can squeeze through tiny gaps and flop down until they are almost flat — their 'doormat' position. Do *not* try treading on a wombat! You'll regret it (and so will the wombat).

Adult wombats are about a metre long, but like humans this varies a lot. Some wombats are relatively small even when they are grown up; others can grow to about 120 centimetres. One of our wombats, Pretty Face, is only the size of a corgi — though she's a different shape. (She also has the prettiest pointed nose and long fluffy whiskers — she's a gorgeous wombat.)

The biggest wombat I have ever known, Chocolate, was taller than my knees, with shoulders like a sumo wrestler's and a broad, flat face, a bit like a hairy-nosed wombat's, but he was just a big common wombat.

The colour of wombats

Wombat skin is white but their fur comes in different colours, just as humans have different coloured hair.

In our valley wombats can be almost black or deep brown or grey or even gold in colour. Some wombats, especially in very cold areas, go almost white in winter, then lose their fluffy winter coats in summer and turn brownish-grey again. Most Tasmanian wombats are grey. Wombats usually go greyer as they get older; some just become paler and paler, so they are gold instead of brown. But I have known young wombats that were grey or gold. (For a while we had a wombat we called the Golden Dragon. He used to bite anyone who walked down the path to our swimming hole in the creek.)

When you look closely at wombat's fur it is really made up of different coloured hairs — a grey wombat will have black and white as well as grey hairs.

Are there any spotted wombats? No, you'll never see a spotted wombat, or a striped wombat, or even a wombat with pretty markings like a horse's or a cat's. But dark wombats can have patches of white fur, and the first wombat I knew well, Smudge, was grey except for a golden smudge across one ear and part of his head.

Wombat fur is very, very coarse — just like a doormat. If a wombat is out in light rain only the top of its fur coat will get wet, so the wombat still stays warm. Even mud usually doesn't stick to wombat fur — though wombats can get pretty dusty.

A wombat's face

Wombats have very strong, flattish skulls — which is a good thing as they use their heads like battering rams. They charge head first through fences, fly-screen doors and kitchen cupboards, and use their heads to tackle any person who stands in their way.

Wombats have tiny eyes that are mostly closed, so grit can't get in them. The only vulnerable bit of a wombat's head is its ears. When wombats fight they try to bite each other's ears. But mostly they try to bite each other's bums. It's a lot easier to grab a wombat's bum than a wombat's head!

Wombats have broad, dry leathery noses — pink when they are young and then dark brown as they get older, and often muddy or dusty! They have very big nostrils. Smelling is the main way a wombat 'sees' the world (see Chapter 8) — when you look at a wombat skull you'll see the nostril openings are enormous.

Wombats have two giant lower teeth and two big upper teeth, well apart from their other teeth. Wombat's teeth keep growing all their lives, and are ground down by the tough tussocks and other things they eat. They have dark narrow lips — wombats can sometimes grin, which means they are 'on heat' (see Chapter 6) or, like humans, are enjoying themselves.

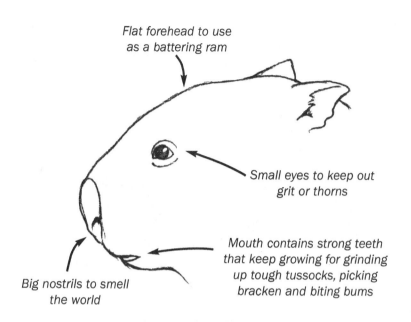

Flat forehead to use as a battering ram

Small eyes to keep out grit or thorns

Mouth contains strong teeth that keep growing for grinding up tough tussocks, picking bracken and biting bums

Big nostrils to smell the world

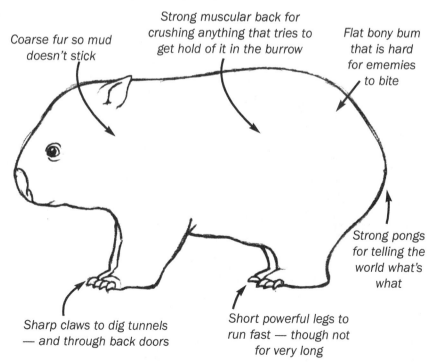

Coarse fur so mud doesn't stick

Strong muscular back for crushing anything that tries to get hold of it in the burrow

Flat bony bum that is hard for ememies to bite

Sharp claws to dig tunnels — and through back doors

Short powerful legs to run fast — though not for very long

Strong pongs for telling the world what's what

front paws

hind paws

A wombat's legs and feet

Wombats have short legs and fleshy pads on their feet, a bit like a dog's paw but broader, and they stand and walk in a very flat-footed manner. Wombats are built for standing around eating and for digging, so they don't stand on tip-toe like animals that run a lot.

The wombat's front feet have five long claws — the more the wombat digs the blunter and shorter the claws get. Some wombats have only tiny claws. Others, like our wombat Big Paws, never dig at all. His claws look like he's been to the beautician and had false nails stuck on.

A wombat's hind legs are longer and narrower, with only four claws on each of its feet. The front feet dig, and the back feet shovel out the dirt behind them.

How fast can a wombat run?

Wombats can run about 40 kph over short distances. I timed Roadbat at 32 kph and Burper at just over 40 kph. Wombats can't run as fast as that for very long — but they can put on a burst of speed to get to their burrow, knocking over anything in the way! Gabby wombat (see Chapter 11) could run at only about 10 kph.

The sex of a wombat

How do you tell the difference between a male and a female wombat? The best way is to turn the wombat over. (Warning: wombats will not like you checking them out. You may lose a few fingers!)

Once a wombat is on its back it's easy to see what sex it is. A male wombat will have testicles — his penis is stored inside his body and it doesn't dangle like that of many other mammals.

A female wombat will have a pouch, but you may have to run your fingers through its fluffy tummy fur to find it. (*Don't* put your fingers in the pouch, though. If there's a tiny baby inside you might hurt it.)

The pouch faces backwards, towards the back legs — that way it doesn't fill up with dirt when the wombat digs. Each pouch has two teats for the baby to drink from. The pouch is pink and pretty hairless, and there is a strong sphincter, or circular muscle, that stops the very small wombat from falling out when the mother runs or jumps.

If you meet a wombat and it growls at you it's probably a female. I'm serious! A female wombat is often much stroppier, especially if she has a baby!

If the wombat has a baby bouncing after it, it's a female. Look underneath the wombat too. If there is a baby in the pouch, the pouch will sag down. Sometimes the pouch stays sagged even after the baby has left, so a droopy tummy indicates it's a female wombat.

The female wombat is usually a bit bigger than the male, too, but wombats vary so much in size that this way of telling them apart doesn't always work. The female often (but not always) has a narrower, pointier face than the male. As the male wombat grows older his head tends to become wider and flatter.

Rikki the Wrestler

I have a scar on my left wrist from a wombat I called Rikki the Wrestler. Rikki *loved* wrestling — most young wombats do, especially males. Rikki used to grab my skirt and pull it until it tore, or he would gallop up behind me and rip my jeans. One day I bent to scratch him (wombats *love* being scratched along the back and behind the ears where it's hard for them to reach). He grabbed my wrist and bit hard.

Blood spurted out everywhere! I screamed and pulled away and Rikki pulled even harder. Hey, this was a *great* game, he thought. Let's wrestle!

The more I shrieked the more he thought I was enjoying myself ... and the more I pulled away the more he tugged too!

I finally managed to get his jaws open.

Rikki never had any idea he had hurt me. He just thought we were both having fun.

3

A Day in the Life of a Wombat

A wombat's day

Wombats go back to their burrows soon after sunrise and that's where they sleep during most of the day. A wombat burrow is the perfect place for a sleeping wombat. No matter how hot or dry it is outside it's always the same temperature and humidity down a wombat burrow.

Wombat holes usually have several 'bedrooms' — chambers with soft, dry dust or a bed of dried grass or bracken on the floor. (One of our wombats, Mothball, picks branches of lavender and drags them to her hole. She has the best smelling wombat bed in Australia!) But some wombat burrows aren't deep enough to have 'rooms', so the wombat sleeps in a hollow just far enough underground to be sheltered from the sun.

Wombats fall asleep on their sides ...

... or curled up ...

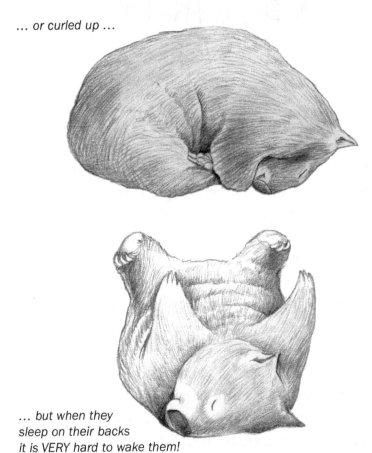

... but when they sleep on their backs it is VERY hard to wake them!

Sometimes the wombat scratches up its bed to make it fluffier, or wriggles down into the dust. Then it sits on its bum and slowly falls asleep. Its eyes close and it sinks down lower and lower until its head rests on the floor too. A wombat's temperature also falls when it's asleep in its burrow.

A wombat can doze standing up but in its burrow it usually first goes to sleep lying on its side, either curled up or stretched out, or on its tummy. After an hour or more the wombat rolls over onto its back, with its legs up in the air — the back legs straight up and the front legs bent a bit.

When a wombat sleeps like this it is very, very sound asleep — sometimes it is in such a deep sleep that it's impossible to wake it!

Sneezy

Sneezy lived in the wombat hole behind our bathroom. She's the only wombat I have ever known to get hayfever. Sometimes as I walked around the garden I'd hear a sneeze deep underground, 'Ah-tchoo!'

One morning I opened the back door. There was Sneezy lying on her back, on the doormat, her legs in the air.

I prodded her with my foot. 'Hey, wake up! I want to go outside.'

Sneezy didn't move.

I prodded her again. 'Wake up, you dingbat wombat!'

Sneezy still didn't move.

I knelt down next to her. What was wrong?

She didn't seem to be breathing! I couldn't feel a heartbeat either. She seemed strangely stiff, as well.

I sat back. Had she died in the night? She'd been fine the night before.

I cried a bit, on the doorstep. I still couldn't work out why she had died. Was there a wombat illness I didn't know of? Had her sneezing been a sign of lung disease?

By coincidence a vet friend was coming for breakfast that morning. Maybe she could look at Sneezy and work out what had happened.

So the vet and I lifted Sneezy up onto the kitchen table. The vet checked Sneezy over carefully, then shook her head. 'I can't see anything wrong. It's a mystery,' she said.

We dug a grave among the orange trees and carried Sneezy down. We lowered her into the grave ...

And Sneezy woke up! One very startled wombat blinked at us, then galloped for her hole behind the bathroom. A faint sound floated up from underground ... 'Ah-tchoo! Ah-tchoo!'

Sneezy wasn't dead! She had been asleep.
It had never occurred to me, or the vet, that
wombats slept so deeply.

Most wombats don't sleep quite as soundly
as Sneezy, but when they are in their deep sleep
stage they can still be very difficult to wake up!

I call Mothball by banging two rocks together at the
front of her burrow. If she is asleep on her tummy or on
her side she'll wake up. But if she is asleep on her back
there's nothing I can do to wake her up.

Just like people, some wombats sleep more deeply
than others.

Towards the end of the afternoon the wombat
wakes up in its bedchamber and moves closer to the
entrance of the burrow, then it goes to sleep again.
But this time it isn't deeply asleep — it's just dozing
and smelling the air and feeling its warmth, and
waiting until it's cool and dark enough to go outside.
The hungrier the wombat is, the earlier it will
venture out.

If it's very cold or raining hard, a wombat will stay
in its burrow all night — sometimes even two nights
in a row if it's a good season and the wombat is fat
and not too hungry. But, no matter what, it'll be out
the third night — even if the rain is still teeming
down.

A wombat's afternoon

Usually wombats stay in their burrows until it gets dark. Too much heat or sunlight can kill a wombat — they can die of heat prostration in ten minutes on a hot sunny day. Sometimes though wombats will sleep on their backs outside their holes on sunny afternoons in mid-winter, when elderly wombats come out to doze in warm dust baths. But even then, if wombats come out in daylight too much, their skin dries out and they are more likely to be infected by the tiny mites called mange that can kill them — or leave them blind and deaf and in agony.

During bad droughts, or if cattle and sheep have eaten all the grass, starving wombats desperate for food will come out during the day, hoping to get a bit more to eat. Sadly these wombats don't live for very long — heat or mange kills them, as well as starvation.

But if you live in a deep valley — like we do — you can watch wombats in the late afternoon from autumn to late spring. It's safe for wombats then — the sun goes behind the ridges and the valley is in shadow. (I spend most of my afternoons watching the wombats through my study window.)

When wombats first come out of their burrows they are a bit sleepy — just like you or me when we first wake up. Sometimes a wombat will sit down and doze for a few minutes before munching a bit more grass. Or maybe the wombat isn't really sleeping, but slowly smelling the air, to see what the weather is like, what food is about, who is doing what and if there is any danger around.

Then a wombat gets down to serious eating. Or serious scratching. Or serious droppings making. Because for a wombat, eating, scratching and leaving droppings are very, *very* serious indeed.

Do wombats have wombat friends?

I don't know. Some wombats do seem to like the company of other wombats — and they probably aren't their own children or wombats they have mated with in the past. Other wombats like being by themselves. But I don't know if they feel the way we do about friends. (I have known a wombat to stand by a dead wombat, killed by a car, for a whole day and night. It wasn't its baby or mother, just a wombat who shared its territory. But this was the only time I have known a wombat to show any sign of grief that another wombat had died — and maybe it wasn't grief at all.)

4

The Wombat Essentials: Eating and Scratching

When you first see a wombat it will probably be either eating or scratching. Sometimes it will be eating *and* scratching. That's how you can tell if a wombat is outside at night too — you'll hear the steady *chomp chomp chomp* interrupted by *scratch scratch scratch*.

What wombats like to eat

If wombats were to be given the choice of every wonderful food in the universe, they'd choose grass — lovely, lush, green grass — and they'd be producing lovely, long, green droppings too.

When there isn't a lot of soft grass about, wombats eat many other things. It depends what's around.

Wombats have long strong teeth, so they can chew up tough sedges and tussocks. They'll eat the bark from young trees and dig up all sorts of roots.

Wombats mostly like the food they are used to — a bit like us. If wombats have been reared by people they'll have been introduced to many different foods, like carrots, sweet potato, corn on the cob, 'wombat nuts' — a bit like a grain and lucerne (alfalfa) biscuit — or rolled oats. Most wombats like rolled oats, even wild wombats.

We had a wombat called Rikki for a while. He went bush, as wombats always do. Then the drought began and it got drier and drier ...

One afternoon there was an 'Aaaark!' at the back door ('Aaark!' is wombat for 'Feed me *now* or I'll bash your door down!').

It was Rikki, and he had four strange wombats with him. So I put some oats in a dish made from an old hubcap my husband Bryan had nailed to a big bit of wood, so Rikki couldn't knock it over — wombats are messy eaters. Then I put down food for the other wombats too. They looked a bit uneasy, as though they weren't quite sure about dropping in on a human for dinner. But they ate the oats.

Every afternoon after that there were five wombats waiting for their dinner. Then there were six ... then seven ...

Luckily it rained then or we might have been

feeding a hundred wombats. Rikki and his mates went bush as soon as the grass grew and we never saw any of them again. But I was always glad that Rikki was able to say to his mates, 'Hey, come on, I know where there's some pretty good tucker!'

Just like us, wombats can be fussy eaters. I've raised wombats that wouldn't touch a carrot, while others would break down the door to get more of them. (I mean they *really* break down the door — we now have a steel-reinforced back door to keep out the wombats!)

Smudge and the apricots

Wombats who live in orchards learn to like fruit. Grunter spends his nights eating windfall apples and pears — we grow a hundred and fifteen different kinds of apples, so there are ripe apples from November to July. (We call him Grunter because all those apples make him burp — and fart ... and Grunter is a more polite name than Farter.)

Smudge, the first wombat I lived with, loved apricots. He sat under the apricot tree waiting for ripe fruit to fall. He munched them carefully, all around the stone. His fur grew sticky and his droppings were squishy and smelt like rotten apricot.

One day I cut six cases of apricots in half and laid them out on sheets of aluminium foil to dry in the sun. Every night I took them inside so they didn't get wet in the dew, then spread them out again next morning.

I came back late from town one afternoon and raced up the hill to bring the apricots inside.

And then I stopped and stared.

There were no apricots to be seen. But there *was* a very stuffed wombat, sitting with his eyes half closed. Every now and then he burped up a smell of apricot.

I didn't see Smudge for two nights after that. And he was never interested in apricots again.

Wombats living in different areas will eat different kinds of foods — and sometimes wombats in the same area will have different favourite foods, too. Flat White loves the stalks of 'blady grass' — a coarse, tussocky plant whose blades are so tough and sharp they cut your hand if you try to pick them, but the lower stems are tender. Flat White manages to chew the bottom bits and leaves the top bits on the ground.

Wombats will often have a nibble, too, of anything around — a bite out of a mushroom, a gnaw at moss on a rock, or a bite from a fallen avocado. But usually it's the younger wombats who experiment with newer tastes — the old ones stick to what they know, unless they are very hungry.

Charlie the chip eater

A friend's two daughters were sitting on the verandah at their house last year, eating a packet of potato chips, when a young wombat bounced up behind them, sniffed the chip packet, then stuck its nose in it.

Its nose came out all covered in chips. The wombat chewed thoughtfully, decided it *liked* potato chips, then grabbed the packet and ran off with it. But that was a very playful wombat. Most wombats, even young ones, are too nervous to approach children, even if they are eating delicious-smelling potato chips.

(By the way, potato chips are bad for wombats — they're too fatty and salty. Too many chips can kill a wombat, which the girls knew — they made sure that they kept their chips out of wombat reach after that!)

Wombats who are hungry, or who have grown up during a drought or in an area where there isn't a lot of good food around, look like they are vacuuming the grass. They stay with their heads down eating steadily. Wombats eating during lush periods are much more fussy. They nose about looking for things they *really* like to eat.

If there is a big sweet patch of grass, or a bowl of wombat nuts, they will sit on their bums to eat. But usually they eat standing up. They'll also travel a long way to find their favourite foods — they'll even dig through snow to find food.

Do wombats drink?

Young wombats drink milk from their mothers. Adult wombats do drink but in lush periods they may get enough moisture from grass and dew. Like most nocturnal animals, wombats usually prefer to drink at dusk soon after they wake up ... and they drink very, *very* slowly!

Wombats usually take the same path to water and drink at the same place. But if there is a strange scent around, like a dog's, they may avoid that drinking spot for days rather than drink where a dog has drunk. Wombats who are more familiar with dog smell seem less worried by a reasonably old scent.

(If you take your dog into the bush, don't let it sniff all around the waterhole. The dog's smell might scare away a wombat who badly needs a drink.)

How to scratch a wombat

Wombats love to scratch. They'll scratch with their front legs or their back legs. They'll rub against trees. They'll sneak under parked cars and scratch their backs on the car's axles — and get very greasy in the process.

They'll rub their backs on garden chairs and tables — usually knocking them over. We have an earthquake every morning at about two o'clock. It's really Mothball scratching her back on the floor joist under our bed — but it *sounds* like an earthquake.

Wombats will stop whatever they're doing to have a scratch — they may be eating steadily or bashing down a door or pushing their way through a fence. Then suddenly they'll stop, as though they have room for only one thing on their mind at a time — and at that precise moment it's an *itch*!

Wombats will often rub up against a post or tree to leave their scent. But mostly it's just because they are itchy — sometimes with mange (see Chapter 11) but often it is just, well, an itch! Some trees and rocks get very dusty, or shiny, if they are rubbed every night by a wombat.

Wombats don't lick or groom themselves, like cats and some other animals do. Sometimes a female wombat will sit on her bum and lean over to lick and groom her pouch area, or scratch it gently, or wriggle her tummy on damp grass.

Wombats who are familiar with humans, *love* to be scratched, especially on the long bony ridge along their back or behind their ears, places they can't quite reach themselves.

The harder a wombat is scratched the better — especially if you rub your boot along its back. Often it

49

will go all weak at the knees and flop down into doormat position, its tummy flat on the ground and its legs stretched out, with a look of wombat bliss on its face.

A wombat will also lie on its back to be scratched, though you have to be gentler this way.

A wombat is not . . .

- a bear (though they look a bit like one)
- a badger (they both live in holes and are hairy but that's about it)
- allowed on the sofa (this means you, Mothball — off!)
- a pet (wombats will *always* be wild animals — they may bite you, growl at you — and need the freedom to wander, dig and have their own wombat lives to be really happy).

Seriously, wombats who become fond of humans may look for humans — and die as they run after cars or dogs or shooters.

5

Wombats and Friends

Wombats don't seem to make friends the way dogs and people do. Most wombats live in a burrow by themselves. Burrows may be used by more than one wombat, but not at the same time. It's a bit like 'time sharing' — they will use the burrow at different times.

Each wombat has a favourite burrow, but it will also have other ones it might visit. The wombat will sniff to see if another wombat is inside, but if it is scared it will just charge right in. Then you'll hear *grlll, chomp!* as the wombat that is already there tries to bite the visitor's nose. Both wombats will race out to fight properly. But if there is a dog outside, or a fox or a human they are scared of, they'll both dash inside again — and this time the first wombat will let the other one stay there, out of danger.

Do wombats share?

Wombats don't have territories the way other animals do. They have an area where they feed most of the time, but other wombats can share this as long as they stay at least two metres away! Sometimes several wombats will eat at the same time (just not nose to nose), but usually one wombat will feed at one time then another wombat later that night.

Wombats are often more tolerant of each other when there's a drought and not much grass for everyone, or when it has rained and there's so much grass that an army of wombats, kangaroos and wallabies couldn't eat it all. But some wombats jealously guard 'their' grass and won't let any other animal near.

Usually young, fit wombats have the 'best' feeding times — early evening and just before dawn. An old, sick wombat may feed in that good grassy area only when other wombats don't want to, such as in the late afternoon when it's still too hot to be comfortable.

If a wombat comes too close to another stroppy wombat there'll be growls and snarls until the intruder backs off. And, it doesn't matter how big a wombat is, or how long its teeth are because the top wombat is the one who is stroppiest and growls longest and loudest!

Some wombats hate *any* animal feeding near them. I have seen Mothball bite a passing wallaby on the leg

Womabats will share their grass with their babies — even when the baby is almost as big as they are. But other wombats have to keep their distance.

because it dared eat grass where she was feeding. Then she chased it right down to the orchard!

Do wombats talk?

Wombats mostly don't use sounds to communicate. They don't learn our words either, like dogs do. I have never known a wombat even to learn its own name — or, at least, the name I've given it. Wombats have very good hearing but they don't process the information they hear very well. They have to think a while to understand they've heard, just like we have to think for a few seconds to work out what we are smelling. Wombats know each other by their smell and the smell of their droppings, not by names.

Baby wombats who are brought up with people will learn that when a person yells there might be food around. But they don't care what words you have used. You can yell, 'Here, wombat!' or 'There's a dead mouse in the sink!' and they'll come just the same.

The wild wombats around where we live don't pay any attention when I call them — they only come for their food when they can smell it, not when I yell for them to come and get it.

Wombats do make a few sounds that you can learn, even though they aren't really words:

Gnug, gnug, gnug means 'Here I am, where are you?' Baby wombats make this sound if their mothers are too far away.

Yip with a snarl can mean 'This is my territory, get lost!' or 'Feed me my carrots immediately!' Or maybe it just means 'Me, wombat! Obey!'

Growlllarf! means 'Get away at once!' If a mother wombat makes this sound when you are near her baby — run!

But if you *really* want to learn how to speak wombat, you'll have to learn a quite different way of communicating (see Chapter 9).

Gossiping wombats

Sometimes wombats meet other wombats as they wander through the bush and just stop, nose to nose. They can stay like that for ten minutes or half an hour. I have *no* idea what they are doing. Gossiping? Exchanging smells? If only my nose was as good as a wombat's, I could 'talk' to them and find out!

Wombat fights: bum biting and battles

Most wombats snarl but don't attack. But wombats can be vicious fighters.

If a wombat wants another wombat to go away, they growl at it first. If that doesn't work they give a high-pitched yell. And if yelling fails the first wombat sneaks up behind the second one (this is a good tactic, because it's hard to smell a wombat that is sneaking up behind you) and bites it on the bum.

The bitten wombat lunges around and tries to bite the first wombat … it runs away … or it just snarls and keeps on eating.

Mostly the wombat who yells the most wins — the other wombat just runs off, as though it doesn't think it's worth arguing. But sometimes wombat battles turn into real fights.

It's hard to attack something that is mostly bone and muscle and tough skin. A fighting wombat tries to tear off an ear or bite its opponent on the nose. It will also try to rip off the other wombat's testicles (if it's a male) — any part that can be grabbed and torn is vulnerable. But usually one wombat retreats before it is badly hurt.

Wombats are more likely to be hurt when they attack each other down wombat burrows. They can't turn around in a narrow hole to present their tough bums to their opponent, and their nose or ears can be badly bitten.

Sometimes wombats just plain hate each other. They'll yell at each other every night until one of them decides to 'leave town'. But mostly they just avoid the wombats they don't get on with.

Moriarty

The stroppiest wombat I ever met was Moriarty.
She was only a small wombat, a bit like a
football with legs — and teeth — but she never
let any other animal near her feeding area.
(Often female wombats with a baby are the
most aggressive and try to keep other wombats
away from their grass.)

Moriarty moved into Smudge's territory when
he died. Smudge had let me follow him about
the bush. He even seemed to like my company.
But if I came too close to Moriarty she bit my
knee.

She didn't like Fred the wallaby bounding
past her either.

'Eeeegh!' snarled Moriarty. She bit Fred's
tail.

'Aaaaaaaaar!' screamed Fred. He leapt
higher than I had ever seen a wallaby leap
before.

'Eeeegh!' growled Moriarty. This was *her*
territory. And no other animal was allowed in it.

Moriarty attacked wombats, wallabies,
echidnas and a king parrot that was silly enough
to land beside her nose. She attacked anything
— including me.

It was my fault. I decided to fence the
vegetable garden — mostly to stop Fred the

wallaby from eating my corn and carrots. But Moriarty's bum was parked exactly where the gate was going to go.

'Hey, you!' I said. 'Move!'

Moriarty kept eating.

'Go away, you dingbat wombat!' I yelled.

'Eeeegh!' snarled Moriarty. She grabbed my boot between her jaws and bit down hard.

Luckily my boots were tough.

'Sorry about this, wombat,' I said. Then I turned the hose on her.

Moriarty bit at the water but found nothing to sink her fangs into. She shot me a damp, disgusted look and dashed for the thornbush. She peered out, angry and bedraggled.

'Eeeegh!' she hissed.

From then on it was war.

I finished the fence that afternoon. Moriarty was locked out of the vegetable garden ... for about ten minutes.

Moriarty dug under the wire.

I weighed the wire down with rocks.

Moriarty burrowed under the rocks.

I buried the wire half a metre deep.

Moriarty burrowed deep down, under the wire.

I filled in her burrow with more rocks.

Moriarty dug those rocks out too.

I then asked a friend to help me move a truckload of giant boulders.

'There's no way any wombat can move these!' declared my friend.

But the next morning the boulders had been shifted — and Moriarty was in the vegetable garden ... again.

How could one small wombat move giant boulders?

That night I stayed up late. But there was no sign of Moriarty.

I stayed up late the second night too. No wombat.

But on the third night a small, round, brown shape padded down to the vegetable garden.

Was that something in her mouth? I peered into the moonlit night. It was a tomato stake!

Even now it's hard to believe what I saw that night. But there in the moonlight Moriarty used that tomato stake as a lever. The rock moved one centimetre, two ... just enough for a furry body to squeeze past.

I have never seen a wombat use a tool again (though I have seen Mothball shift a box so she could stand on it to attack the mop!).

I gave up after that. I started another vegetable garden beyond the creek. Moriarty had won the war.

Moriarty died seven years later, in the vegetable garden, grey and thin and crusted with scabs from mange. Even then she glared at me, daring me to try to help her. She would have used her last breath to bite me.

She's buried where she died. A slow death from age and mange is not a death you'd wish on any enemy.

After she died a black-tailed wallaby — Fred's successor — began grazing in the old vegetable garden, munching with glee the young oats springing up from the mulch. I wondered how long he had been waiting, looking longingly at the feast, intimidated by Moriarty, the meanest wombat I have known.

6

Wombats
Growing Up

When a wombat is a baby it is the cuddliest, most playful creature in the universe.

In our valley baby wombats are mostly born in autumn, and the baby comes out of the pouch around August. But in hotter, drier areas baby wombats are born in summer so that they can feed on grass in the cooler, gentler winter. And in cold areas like Tasmania baby wombats may not be born until mid-winter so that in several months' time they can start to graze on the soft, sweet spring and summer grasses. Sometimes even here we have a wombat born in summer, or in late winter, so we don't see the baby until it emerges from the pouch after Christmas.

A wombat at 3–4 months, attached to mother's teat

A wombat at 6–7 months, heading out of mother's pouch

A wombat's growth cycle

A human baby takes about nine months to be born into the world. A baby wombat is only twenty days old when, as a tiny, hairless, pink blob, it crawls up its mother's fur to her pouch and attaches itself to the teat and starts sucking.

At 3–4 months the baby wombat is still attached to its mother's teat. It has fur on its ears and you can make out its nose and mouth.

The mother wombat's pouch is bigger now. She sometimes growls at other wombats who come close.

If the mother dies when the baby is so young, and if expert human carers look after it, the baby may survive — but it will take a *lot* of love and care. The baby now weighs about 250 grams.

At 6 months the baby moves about the pouch. Its body is still pink and its nose and feet are an even brighter pink. It peers out of the pouch sometimes, but all you really see is a bright pink nose peeping from between its mother's legs.

At 7–8 months the pouch droops right down close to the ground.

By now the baby gets out of the pouch sometimes in the burrow. But it still stays *very* close to Mum.

It sleeps on top of her head, or draped over her body, or next to her.

When the mother goes out to graze, the baby puts its head out between her back legs and has a taste of grass too. Then it does a somersault and pokes its back legs out to urinate. Wombats don't wear nappies! If you spend your life in a pouch you have to work out *some* way of having a wee without getting wet!

The baby is now quite large — about three kilograms or even bigger. It drinks a lot of milk and there is a lot of urine!

At 9–10 months the baby spends nearly all the time out of the pouch.

The baby's nose is still pink, though not as bright as before, but the soles of its feet are darker and the fur is darkening too. It's a brown wombat now, not a pink one. It usually still drinks milk from the long teat in its mother's pouch, but mostly it doesn't bother to get back into the pouch when it wants a snack.

The baby is still scared of strange noises. If frightened, it darts back to Mum or to the burrow. Mum usually keeps fairly close by at this stage, too. As long as the baby isn't startled, though, this is a very playful time — the baby is still well fed with milk so it doesn't need to graze as steadily as its mother; it has lots of time and energy to bounce at shadows, leap out at passing wallabies or tame humans, or sniff how the universe smells. The baby leaves its own droppings now, but usually hides them under a bush.

This is the time when a baby wombat will sometimes play with people. It wants to play with *someone* and Mum is usually too busy eating.

Playing games with wombats

The first wombat baby I ever played with was Sneezy's baby Lurk. I woke up to a din.

Clang, clang, banga, banga, clang, crash, whomp!

Was the house falling down? I looked outside. It was Lurk on the patio.

Clanga, clanga, clanga! Lurk bashed the screen door to set it swinging.

Banga, banga, banga! Lurk jumped on the bouncinette and got it clattering.

Whomp, whomp, whomp! Lurk attacked the rocking chair, then raced back to bash the door again before it stopped swinging.

'Hoy,' I yelled.

Lurk gave a bounce as though to say, 'Come on! Let's play!'

'No way,' I said. 'I'm going back to bed.'

But I did play with him a few nights later.

I wandered down to the orange trees in the moonlight to pick some fruit for breakfast. Suddenly something bashed my knees from behind, almost knocking me down.

It was Lurk.

'What's going on?' I demanded, and then I realised.

Lurk wanted to play.

It was a simple game. Lurk hid behind a bush and jumped out at me, then I hid behind a bush and jumped out at him. The trouble is that wombats are much better at jumping out at humans than humans are at jumping out at wombats.

We played the hide and seek game often after that, dancing at each other in the moonlight. I have played it with other wombats since. Baby wombats *love* to play. Some are timid and will run to Mum if there's a strange noise. But others will play with you for hours as long as you let them get used to your smell first.

At 12–15 months the baby stops drinking milk, but this varies a lot. Sometimes they just stop; other times they may drink every few days or still want to drink but the mother discourages them by lying flat on the ground or gives them a nip.

Baby wombats will sometimes make friends with people at this stage — they still want to play, are very curious and haven't learned that humans can hurt them.

They also start roaming further from Mum and the burrow. About this time many wombats start marking territory, leaving tiny soft droppings around the house, on stairs or on rocks. But others still tactfully hide their droppings away from adult wombats just in case the bigger wombat tries to chase them away.

At about 18 months Mum may take off, leaving junior behind, or junior may wander off instead — or Mum may take junior for walkies and come home without him.

By now the baby looks much like an adult wombat (though it will keep growing for about another year) but its face is finer featured, with a longer-looking nose and softer whiskers. Its bum isn't as rounded and its tail is more prominent than it will be when it's quite grown up. But bum shape varies a lot from wombat to wombat — and in good seasons all wombat bums are pretty fat and round.

Most young wombats dig a bit at this age, but they rarely make a complete burrow — or one that works (see Chapter 7). Any freshly dug dirt will attract them, and they love tearing off bits of shrubbery too.

At 2 years old the young wombat is independent. It might wander far off into a new territory (more often where I live they stay close by and their territory overlaps with their mother's). This depends on the season — in bad seasons all wombats stay close to the best feeding grounds. Baby wombats are more likely to roam further afield in good years.

At 2–3 years the wombat now looks adult and acts adult. It marks its territory with its droppings and uses them to communicate in other ways too. Mostly the wombat moves about a familiar area, well marked with its own scent, though other wombats may wander in this area as well. It is about this time that it starts to mate.

Wombats mating

Wombats have a very long, very noisy, very smelly sex life.

Female wombats go 'on heat' just like dogs do — the time when they are able to become pregnant if they mate. When an animal goes on heat it can only conceive in those few days.

A female wombat on heat will leave oily drops along with her droppings, and the oily stuff may be dropped as she walks too, or rubbed on tussocks or rocks or trees. The drops are very, very smelly — even I can smell them about a hundred metres away, so wombats can probably smell them *kilometres* away!

Most wombats in our valley mate in late winter, but this varies a lot. If it's been really dry and then it rains in mid-summer a few wombats may go on heat a month or two afterwards when they've been eating good, green grass for a while.

Male wombats chase the females for about three days before the female agrees to mate. For years I thought the females were trying to run away, but then I saw Flat White, one of the female wombats in our garden, yip at Big Paws, to get him to chase her. (He wasn't interested.)

If the male catches the female during this time he might bite her — or she might bite him, or chase him, too, though this doesn't happen as much.

For the first couple of days it looks as though the wombats are really angry with each other. But on the last day they look more like they are playing — they nip and chase each other, then the female darts back into her burrow and the male follows her. (Once the deed is done the male comes out soon after and starts to feed and so does the female and they ignore each other from then on.)

I watched Flat White and Big Paws mate this year. They were under my bedroom — which for them was

probably like being in a wombat burrow, but I was able to see them. They lay curled on their sides with the male behind the female, holding her with all four paws around her chest and bum. This lasted for about five seconds the first time, then about a minute the second time.

Around our region, many wombats have a baby about every three years, but some females only ever have one. (Two-and-a-Half wombat had a new baby every eighteen months or so.) A drought or lush year doesn't have any effect on breeding — there are as many babies in pouches in droughts as there are in lush years. But this may be different in drier areas, where the wombats don't get as much to eat. (Even in droughts here the wombats are able to eat the fallen fruit — Grunter loves apples and pears, and Big Paws and Pretty Face adore avocadoes.)

Most wombats don't go on heat again until the baby has left home completely, though this isn't always the case. Two-and-a-Half sometimes had a baby in her pouch and a baby bouncing beside her.

A stubborn baby wombat

Sometimes baby wombats don't *want* to get out of the pouch.

Three years ago Mothball wombat's pouch got bigger and bigger and *bigger*. It finally got so big it was dragging on the ground — Mothball's baby, Hark, was so large that he didn't fit in the pouch anymore! So for a while we had a two-headed wombat. There was Mothball's head at one end eating grass. And, there at the other end, was Hark's head poking out between Mothball's back legs eating grass too.

Then Hark did a somersault and his back legs poked out instead, then a great arc of urine flew up into the sky. Hark was drinking a *lot* of milk by now, so there was a *lot* of urine.

Finally Mothball worked out how to get her stubborn baby out of her pouch.

I glanced out my study window one afternoon just as Mothball trotted up to the herb garden with a determined look on her face.

Mothball leapt up at the garden wall! *Whump!* Her pouch bashed against the low stone wall.

Mothball leapt at the wall again. *Whump!*

Hark poked his head out of the pouch. He looked slightly stunned.

Mothball leapt a third time. *Whump!*

That was it! Hark crawled out of the pouch. He gazed around nervously as though to say, 'This world is big!'

Mothball igored him. She began to eat grass. A few minutes later Hark began to eat too.

Ten minutes later the baby decided that it was time for a nap. He started to stick his head

back in the pouch and … *Thud!*

Mothball flopped flat on the grass on her tummy. Hark tried to wriggle under her, to get back in. But Mothball wasn't moving.

They were still munching grass together when I went out to pick some beans for dinner. I bent down and began to hunt through the bean bushes.

Whump! Something dived head first down my jumper. Then it did a somersault. A small brown face peered up out of my jumper as though to say, 'Aha! A *big* wombat pouch!' (Never lean over when there's a baby wombat about!)

For a while Hark padded at Mothball's heels. Then he grew bolder. He bounced at wallabies and echidnas. He bounced at shadows and loved to play the hide and seek game that I'd first played with Lurk.

One afternoon I looked out to see Mothball padding determinedly up the mountain, with Hark at her side.

Two days later Mothball was back, but there was no sign of Hark. Mothball had decided it was time that he was weaned. Hark did return a year later, though. He and Mothball don't have much to do with each other now. They just sniff each other vaguely as they pass, as though to say, 'Hey, I did know you once, didn't I?'

7

The Secret World Underground

Wombats are great diggers, but they are *lousy* engineers!

Most young wombats dig a little — a bit like children playing in a sandpit. But those holes mostly collapse, or the baby wombat gets bored. In all the time I've studied wombats Mothball is the only one who dug a new hole that didn't collapse ... and even that filled up with water when it rained!

Most wombats renovate old burrows. A wombat moves into a hole that hasn't been used for months or years. They clear out any dirt that has fallen into the passages. They haul in new bracken or tussocks to make a bed.

This means that wombats live in burrows that have been dug ten, fifty, one hundred years before —

or maybe thousands of years ago. So if wombats are going to move into a new area there have to be wombat holes already there for them to shelter in! If the old holes have been destroyed by farming or logging and there aren't any wombats about that are good engineers, there won't be any new burrows for them to move into, maybe for decades.

The soil has to be right for wombat burrows, too — heavy soil that can be compacted into hard walls, with rocks or tree roots to help support the entrance. You can't dig a good burrow in sand! Burrows also collapse if there are too many cattle in a paddock with their heavy bodies on small hard feet, or if the land is ploughed.

Wombats also dig under fences. this doesn't need much engineering skill and all wombats are pretty good at it.

What's it like down a wombat burrow?
Wombat burrows are fascinating! There are passages that go deep into the hill ... and rooms where you can sit up.

When I was younger — and thinner — I used to wriggle down wombat holes. These days zoologists can put miniature trackers or cameras on wombats to see what happens deep underground. But in those days the only way to find out was to crawl down there myself.

narrow entrance

'bedroom'

S-bend to catch water

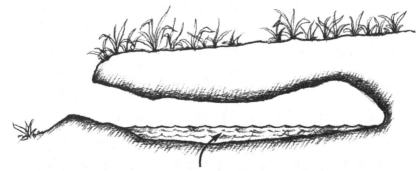

water fills a straight burrow

I was nervous the first time. Would I get stuck and never be able to get out? Would I meet a snake? What if the hole collapsed? What if I couldn't turn round?

But it wasn't like that at all. As soon as I got inside, the hole dipped down, then up again. Then it opened into a tiny room. I could sit up and shine the torch around.

The walls were hard and the floor was soft fine dust. At one end of the room the 'door' led to another tunnel. I lay down on my tummy again and kept on wriggling.

After about a metre I came to another room. This one was even bigger. And it had a 'bed' too, made of a pile of dry bracken and tussocks, for the wombat to sleep on.

The burrow became narrower after that, so I didn't go any further. But the other wombat burrows I have been down were much the same — 'hallways' then 'rooms'. Sometimes there would be passages off to one side, occasionally with old wombat bones in them.

The deep wombat burrows around our valley go hundreds of metres into the hillsides and have lots of entrances. Others in sheltered spots, like the one Mothball lives in under our bedroom, are only about two metres long.

Most wombats have a favourite burrow, but they sometimes visit other ones. Other wombats share three or four burrows with different wombats — not at the same time, but on a time-share arrangement (see Chapter 5).

Different types of wombat burrows

The perfect wombat burrow has a narrow entrance, to discourage dogs and foxes. It dips down then rises up again, so water can't flow down it — a bit like an S-bend in a toilet!

Other wombat burrows just go straight in, and when it rains water rushes down them in an underground stream, or they collapse.

The perfect wombat burrow has great big rooms with soft dry sand, and several entrances so that the wombat can travel safely underground, or escape if there is danger.

But you hardly ever find the perfect wombat burrow, just as you don't find the perfect house either!

The wombat hole in a cave

Once when Bryan and I were caving we came upon a very startled wombat! This wombat had made the caves her home. Some of the caves were big enough for us to stand up — a wombat palace!

Roadbat wombat used to live in the pipes under the road. The pipes were cool and sheltered him from the sun — what more did he need? Every time it rained and the pipes filled up with mud he used to dig them out again. But most wombats are conservative. They like traditional wombat burrows!

When do wombats dig?

Young wombats are mostly enthusiastic diggers. But by the time they are about two years old, or have had their first baby, they are more interested in food than digging. But some wombats like digging all their lives.

Nearly all young wombats start to dig a few holes, and nearly all wombats will do lots of digging to renovate the old holes they move into. Sometimes a bare patch of dirt will tempt them to dig. If I dig a new flowerbed some dingbat wombat is sure to start a hole there, but usually wombats love to dig after rain, when the ground is soft and holds together well — perfect hole-digging weather!

Wombats also dig because they are angry, to mark their territory, to renovate their holes or make them bigger, or to make themselves comfortable. But sometimes they dig just because the fresh dirt smells good. Humans sing or do other things if they are happy, or sad, or bored. Well, wombats dig!

(P.S. I just looked through the window. Mothball has dug up the grass all around her feeding bowl. I forgot to feed her last night, so this is the Revenge of the Wombat!)

How wombats get their own burrows

When young wombats want a burrow of their own they look for an empty one — one where the former wombat has died or moved out. Most wombats die deep underground, so the new wombat scratches out all the bones and any old bedding or bits of collapsed ceiling. Then they carry in new bracken or grass for their bed and leave their droppings all about so other wombats know that this is now their place.

Sometimes a really stroppy newcomer will force another wombat out of its burrow so it can live there — either by lots of snarling and yelling or after a real battle (see Chapter 5). But most wombats don't like fighting. If a stroppy wombat demands a burrow, then the other wombat just leaves!

Sometimes wombats will dig a new front door for an old hole. I wandered down to one of our paddocks a few weeks ago and there was a great pile of dirt — next to a new entrance to a giant ancient wombat hole that I never guessed was under my feet. There hadn't been a wombat in that hole for at least 30 years — maybe a lot longer. Horses and cattle feet had destroyed the old entrance long ago. But somehow the new wombat had worked out that somewhere down there was a new wombat palace.

The wombat burrow in a tree

Wombats live in holes in the ground. Koalas live in trees. But once I found a wombat burrow in a tree.

It was a giant dead tree. It had been hit by lightning years before and the top had broken off. The wombat hole started under the roots, then wound up the trunk of the tree — the wombat had dug away the old wood, just as though it was dirt.

The hole finished at the top, about six metres up. The wombat had levelled off a platform to sit on and to look out over the valley.

But wombats are short-sighted and can't see very far (see Chapter 8). Why on earth would a wombat want to look out over the valley?

It took me years to work it out …

8

Wombat Intelligence

Wombats are different from people. I don't just mean they are fat and furry and stand on four legs. Wombats think and see the world in a different way from human beings — and from dogs and other animals too. And their intelligence is different from ours.

How wombats 'see' the world

Human beings usually learn about the world by what it looks or sounds like. We mostly process information that we see or hear. That makes for fast reactions: see a tiger charging, run.

But wombats see and learn about the world by the way it smells. They have to stop and think about what they've smelled as well. A wombat would be a hundred times better as a tracker than a dog and a thousand times better than you — if anyone could ever train a wombat!

Mothball can smell when I've put out her oats two hundred metres away. She can pick out where I walked ten minutes ago, even if I've walked over that spot a hundred times in the past two days.

Wombats sit on a hill and 'see' the view by smelling it. When we look at a view we can only see what it looks like now. But when a wombat 'smells' a view they can smell what was happening yesterday … and the day before … and maybe weeks ago.

How well can wombats see?

Wombats are short-sighted — they mostly focus on dirt and grass. But wombats can function quite well without eyesight. Rikki the Wrestler lost an eye when he was about eighteen months old and then the other one a year later. Maybe he'd been injured fighting, or he'd run into a thorn bush. But it didn't seem to matter — he 'saw' the world with his sense of smell.

How smart are wombats?

Wombats are quite smart — but their sort of intelligence is different from humans.

One of the common ways to test animals for intelligence and memory is to put them in a maze and measure how long it takes them to find their way to food or freedom and then to measure how accurately they remember the maze on subsequent attempts.

If you put a rat (or a person or a dog) in a maze, they'll race around working out how to get out. But a wombat will either just sit there or try to bash the walls down. When you are built like a small, hairy tank, it makes sense either just to sit still if there is danger or to try to crash through it. If a wombat could smell its way out it would be a champion. So a person looks at the wombat just sitting there and thinks, *dumb animal*. But it's not. I suspect that wombats are as intelligent as dogs. But their intelligence is so different from ours that we mostly don't understand it.

A wombat using tools

Moriarty could use a lever and Mothball was able to push a box over to the wall so she could climb up and attack the mop. But I have never seen any other wombats try to use tools. Wombat paws aren't made to hold things, though wombats can carry sticks in their mouths.

How wombats hear the world

Wombats hear very well, but it takes them a while to work out what they are hearing.

It's like the way we smell things. If you smell something rotten it takes you about forty-five seconds to work out what you're smelling ... *I think I can smell something ... yes, I can ... oh, yes, yuk!*

Wombats are like that when they hear something. If a wombat hears a car it thinks, *Can I hear something? Yes, I can ... What is it? Oh, yes, it's a car, I'd better run* ... But by that time the car has hit them. (That's why so many wombats are run over — they literally run under the cars because they have only just worked out what is happening!)

The cleverest wombat of all

For a while we cared for a wombat named Pudge. She was small and round and the most intelligent wombat I have known.

It took Pudge only one night to realise that carrots grew in the vegetable garden. The second night she burrowed under the fence and ate every single carrot.

The third night she worked out that if carrot roots were yummy, celery and parsley roots might taste fantastic.

They did. So did parsnip roots, lettuce roots, ginseng and ginger. Pudge didn't like tomato roots — she just uprooted the tomato bushes to see what they smelled like, then ignored them.

Bryan dug a deep trench around the vegetable garden and filled it with reinforcing mesh. That kept Pudge out of the vegetables. But somehow she managed to spread the word to every other wombat in the district that parsley root was the best tasting stuff since grass.

How did she tell them? I don't know.

Like all wombats, Pudge understood the world by the way it smelled.

I once upset Pudge by taking off my gumboots in front of her. She thought I had split in two. One bit stayed still, the other walked away. She sat and pondered that one for minutes ...

Wombats can learn, but you can't teach them anything — wombats only absorb the information they find useful. You can't teach wombats to come when you call, 'Here, wombat!' — though they may *choose* to come.

But wombats can count. I first tested this with Pudge. She expected two carrots every night. But one night I had only one carrot left.

Pudge ate the carrot then bashed up the garbage bin for half an hour until she realised that no more carrots were coming out the back door.

The second night I decided to see what she'd do if I cut one carrot in two. Pudge ate both halves ... and didn't bash the garbage bin. It was the 'two' that mattered, not the amount of carrot.

How many carrots could Pudge recognise?

Each night for the next week I cut her carrot into three pieces. Then one night I only gave her two whole carrots, instead of one carrot cut into three.

'Arrk!' Pudge attacked the garbage bin until I put out her rightful carrot ration again.

Finally Pudge was counting to six bits of carrot — and yelling if I only put out five. By that time she was wandering off regularly. Her visits to us became fewer and fewer, so I was never able to see exactly how many she could count up to.

Maybe wombats can count to ten ... or twenty or thirty. Maybe I just had a genius wombat, and no other wombat can count to two. Perhaps wombats could do algebra if they thought there was a carrot in it for them. I still haven't been able to find out.

9

How Wombats Talk: Smells and Droppings

Wombats 'talk' to each other with their droppings and other smells. (Life would be a lot smellier if humans talked like wombats.)

Wherever you go in wombat territory you'll see wombat droppings, or scats — usually on the highest rock or log around.

A wombat dropping is a way of saying, 'I live here!' But it says lots of other things too. Sadly, as I'm not a wombat, I can't 'read' wombat droppings very well. But from watching wombats I have a pretty good idea that droppings tell them more than just 'so-and-so was here'.

Small wombats leave small droppings, usually pointed at one end. Large wombats leave giant ones — the bigger the wombat, the bigger the droppings. A wombat can leave a hundred droppings a night.

Wombat droppings don't stink — even if you pick one up and sniff it. Wombats mostly eat grass so their droppings smell like grass too — just a bit digested.

In a drought when there isn't much grass, or the grass is tough and brown, wombat droppings are dark brown to black and shaped like squares, sometimes joined together like building blocks. This is a great shape if you want your dropping to stay on a rock — round droppings would fall off, but square droppings just sit there. (Sometimes the droppings look too fat ever to have fitted through a wombat's bum!)

Where do wombats put their droppings?
When the grass is lush, wombat droppings are green and slightly sloppy — they are dropped wherever the wombat happens to be. Most of the time, though, wombat droppings are placed very, very carefully.

Baby wombats who are still suckling milk but also eating a bit of grass just deposit their droppings anywhere. Sometimes you'll see a tiny line of them that the baby has dropped before it climbs back into its mother's pouch. Baby wombats also produce a *lot* of urine, as they live on milk. (Adult wombats urinate, but not very much, at the same time as they leave a dropping.)

As baby wombats get older, though, they hide their droppings under a bush or zucchini leaf. You have to

When the grass is dry and brown, wombat droppings are brown too, and squarish.

When the grass is lusher, wombat droppings are softer and joined together.

Baby wombats leave tiny pointed droppings. Sometimes they hide them under a bush.

hunt to find them and may wonder if the baby has left the area.

Older wombats use their droppings as a way of communicating or marking their territory. Many droppings will be placed on the highest point around, especially if the wombat is female, though males will do this too. If droppings have been placed on the ground males will often make long scrapes next to them. Sometimes females do this, especially if there are strange wombats about that they have been trying to chase off.

Wombats also leave droppings on any newly dug dirt. I have no idea if this is to say, 'Hey, this dirt is mine!' or 'Hey, nice smell!'

Any new thing in a wombat's territory will probably have a wombat dropping placed on it overnight — if Bryan makes a new rock garden, it's decorated next morning with a large pile of wombat droppings. Fallen branches, new shoes outside the back door, a new doormat — all will be greeted with not just one dropping but a neat pile.

We have to warn visitors about the wombat droppings on the doormat or front steps. Droppings squelching between your toes or under your boot are one of the hazards of living at our place.

In summer, dung beetles break the droppings up in a day or two. In winter the wombat droppings freeze, so they crunch rather than squish. Frozen wombat droppings don't turn into soil until they melt, and so by spring there are a lot of them about, and you have to be careful where you walk for a while.

One morning recently I found wombat droppings on my gumboots and a large pile on the tyres where the zucchini grow — Mothball leaves a dropping there every night, carefully balanced on the tyre.

The droppings aren't just territory markers. Each pile will tell another wombat who left it, their hormonal and emotional state, how old they are, and possibly — probably — many other things that I just don't have sufficient wombat intelligence to work out.

What can you tell from wombat droppings?

- Is the dropping brown, black or green? Can you see bits of grass, seeds or tussock in it? That will tell you what the wombat has been eating.
- Is the dropping soft and squishy or squarish? That will tell you how good a season it is. If there is a lot of grass the droppings will be sloppy; if they're really hard and dry looking, there's a drought.
- Is the dropping on a high point or hidden? Every month or so Mothball leaves droppings all around our house, about a metre apart. This is her way of saying, 'This place is mine.' (No, I am not going to do the same thing — if she wants to claim the house, it's fine by me.)
- Is the dropping tiny, big or enormous? A tiny

dropping means a tiny wombat. If the wombat
dropping is as big as a brick, there's a *Diprotodon*
about. *Run!*

Other good wombat smells

Wombats stink. Sometimes they stink more than
other times. (Dogs find me a very interesting person
to sniff — I always have a faint wombat smell on my
shoes and clothes.)

Wombats learn a lot about each other from the way
their droppings smell. But their other pongs say a lot
too. Many animals produce pheromones — special
scents. (Humans do too — we can't consciously smell
each other's pheromones, but they do affect how we
think about and behave towards each other.)

A wombat's smell probably tells another wombat
a *lot*, including if a wombat is on heat (ready to
mate).

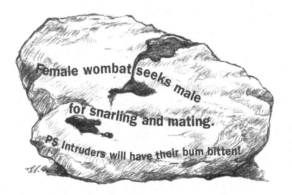

Female wombat seeks male for snarling and mating.

PS Intruders will have their bum bitten!

Wombat droppings can mean many things

10

How to Meet a Wombat

Most people see wombats in zoos — bored, sleepy animals that have too little room to do all the interesting things that wombats can get up to in the wild.

If you really want to meet a wombat, playing wombat games and leading a real wombat life, you have to go bush — and you have to watch them at night or in late afternoon on winter days.

Many people see the bush with lots of other people — a party of bushwalkers or a school excursion. While these are fun — and you can learn a lot — you won't see many animals and, if you do, they'll mostly be running away.

The best way to see animals in the bush is not to tramp through it. Find a quiet place and sit there, to let the animals get used to your scent, and just see what happens.

Return to that spot often to learn more about it. Wombats will be out at different times during the year, and the way they behave depends on whether there has been a drought or a good season; how old they are; if there's lots of grass, and if it's rich summer grass or dry winter grass, which isn't very good tucker; if they have a baby; or if they want to mate; and other reasons. So you need to know an area over a number of years to understand how these animals behave.

How to find a wombat in the bush

1. Look for droppings (scats).
This is the easiest way to see if a wombat is around. If there are wombats about, you'll soon see scats on the highest, most obvious spot a wombat can reach with its bum.

After a while you'll learn to recognise who has left which dropping, or if there has been a strange wombat about. You'll also learn how to tell other things from wombat droppings:

- Is the dropping still dampish? Then the wombat has been around in the last few hours.
- Is the dropping fuzzy from dung beetles? Then it's more than twelve hours old.
- Is it dry and light? It might be two days old, or even weeks old.

2. Smell for wombat odours.

Once you learn what a wombat smells like the pong is unmistakeable! Wombats on heat (see Chapter 6) have a *very* strong odour. But all wombats have a definite smell.

3. Look for wombat scratches.

Wombats will scratch in fresh dirt or where they've left their droppings. But when you're a beginning wombat watcher it's hard to tell if they were made by a wombat or a rabbit. Rabbit scratches are usually narrower and the bottom of the small holes they dig look pointed.

4. Look for wombat burrows.

This isn't the best way to tell if there is a wombat about — the burrow may have been empty for years. Look for fresh digging around its entrance, paw prints, scratches and droppings. If the leaf litter at the front is undisturbed and there is grass growing there that hasn't been tramped down, either the burrow is empty or the wombat is using another entrance.

If you're not sure if there is a wombat inside rake the dirt neatly in front of the hole. Look for prints the next day. If there are big and small prints a mother and baby may live in the burrow.

5. Look for wombat 'sits'.

Wombats often have spots where they sit to 'smell' a view. The ground will be worn bare by the wombat's

A dog's paw print   *A wombat's front paw print*

bum. These spots are often high on a ridge or hill. There won't be droppings there, but there will be nearby.

6. *Look for dust or sand baths.*
These are places where a furry animal has rolled in the dust. Old wombats love to roll in warm dust on winter days — I think it helps their aches and pains (wombats can get arthritis). In hot, dry periods wombats also dig baths in wet sand to cool them down or soothe the itch from mange.

7. *Look for wombat tracks.*
A wombat's front paw print looks a bit like a dog print; the back print looks a bit like a very small human footprint. When a wombat is trudging along normally the front and back prints are close together, but when they are running they will be further apart.

You'll find wombat tracks in sand by creeks, on bare soft dirt, or beside wombat burrows. The prints will also tell you if the wombat has been ambling along, standing to eat, crouching down to drink, or running away from danger.

8. *Look for wombat bones.*
Most wombats die in their burrows, but a few years later the burrow will be 'spring cleaned' by another wombat — and dogs and foxes and goannas may drag the bones out too. You can tell a wombat skull by the two long front teeth in the upper and lower jaws, with smaller teeth much further back.

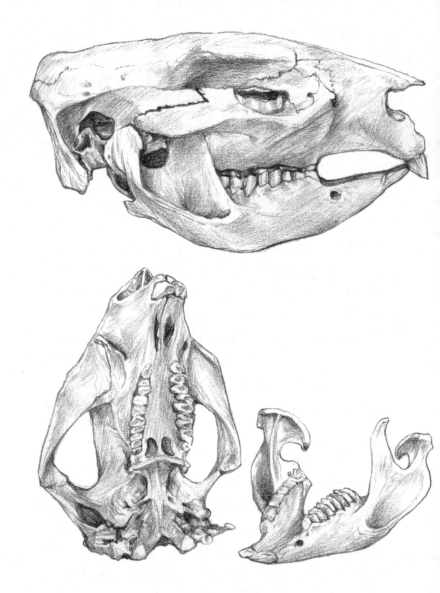

A wombat skull

9. Listen for wombat noises.

Wombats are noisy eaters — you'll hear them going *chomp, chomp, chomp*! They are also noisy scratchers, as they have hard skin, long claws and hair like a shaggy doormat — and they scratch often.

You also hear grunts, huffs, snarls and yips if they are mating and sometimes burps, farts, sneezes, coughs and other wombat noises — but the sound of scratching and the noise of grass or tussock being torn by wombat teeth carries fifty metres or more on a still night.

10. Keep watch for wombats.

Wombats are creatures of habit. If a wombat comes to a certain pool to drink at dusk or a particular patch of grass to eat at one o'clock in the morning, or uses a special branch to scratch, you'll probably find them there the next night — or even the next month. (But probably not the next year.)

Wombats like familiar smells and have favourite bits of grass. But, like humans, they also like routine.

Why you should sing to wombats

Years ago I accidentally discovered how you can get really close to wombats without scaring them away.

I was living in a shed in the bush at the time, mostly by myself. And because there was no-one around to yell, 'Shut up!' I sang to myself as I worked in the orchards.

I noticed that if I walked through the bush the wombats ran away as soon as I came close, but if I sang and walked slowly they just went on eating. I could come right up to them, or sit and watch what they were doing.

How come? Well, wombats aren't scared of humans, but they are *very* easily startled. If you yell, 'Hey, there's a wombat!' and run up to a wombat it will race away in shock.

But if you stand still and let it smell you, the wombat will slowly come closer to investigate — or just ignore you and go about its business of eating or drinking.

And if you sing to a wombat they know where you are, so you don't startle them. It doesn't matter what you sing — just keep singing softly. I know it sounds weird. But it works. And it's how I have been able to spy on the secret lives of wombats for so long.

(Note: Other music doesn't work, so don't try bringing in a rock band. Wombats (mostly) don't enjoy music or even notice it. They just like it when you sing because they know exactly where you are and what you're doing. And if you really hate singing, recite poetry instead — soothingly.)

What to do if you meet a wombat

If you meet a wombat there are things you should know to do.

1. Stand very still, and just watch. The bush is the wombat's home, so don't disturb it. You wouldn't like a stranger to peer in at you while you were having dinner or watching television at your house, so respect a wombat's privacy.

2. If you *really* want to take a closer look, start singing, reciting or chanting very softly. It doesn't matter what you sing, as long as you keep singing. After about three minutes walk very, very slowly towards the wombat, singing as you go. Go one step, count to sixty, then take another step, still singing.

3. If the wombat growls at you, or looks like it might run, or looks puzzled — it doesn't want you there. Walk backwards, not quite so slowly and still singing, so the wombat knows you are going away. But if the wombat wants to play, it will let you know!

4. Never try to pat a wombat — you may lose a finger! If you know the wombat pretty well you can scratch along its back with your boot. (A wombat can't bite your toes if you wear boots — and any snakes around can't bite you either.) But *never* do this with a wombat who isn't used to being around people.

5. Don't approach a wombat that's carrying a baby or has a baby nearby — even if it's a wombat you have met before. (If the wombat wants to say'hi' or be scratched, it will come up to *you*. But even if the wombat decides to approach you with its baby, be very, very careful and don't move suddenly.)

6. Never have a dog with you when you approach a wombat — even a well-trained dog may run after a wombat if it races off. The dog's smell may scare the wombat too, and keep scaring it for days, so it stays away from the food or water that it needs.

7. Don't ever think that a wombat would make a good pet. They don't. Wombats are wild animals — but sometimes people are lucky enough to share their lives and homes with them.

How to tell if there's a wombat in the house

- There's a hole through the back door.
- Your carrots have been eaten, and your rolled oats too.
- Your homework has been torn to shreds (a wombat ate my homework, Sir).
- Someone has tried to dig through the potted plant in the living room and the laundry basket in the bathroom.
- There's a wombat dropping on the coffee table.
- The house smells of eau de wombat.
- Chomp! The wombat has just decided to tell you that it's time for more carrots.

11

Caring for an Orphan Wombat

If a mother wombat has been killed by a car or a dog, or has been shot, the baby in its pouch might still be alive. Sometimes baby wombats are rescued and taken to people who have been trained to look after injured wild animals.

It is an enormous amount of work and responsibility to look after a baby wombat. They must be fed every two hours and kept warm and clean. It can also be heartbreaking, as an orphan wombat may have been hurt when its mother was killed, and will be in shock, and can very easily die.

But a baby wombat is a wonderful cuddly animal, and most fascinating to live with — if you don't mind wombat droppings in your wardrobe and chewed-up toilet paper. Above all you have the incredible privilege of sharing your life for a while with a wild animal.

When an orphan wombat is about a year old it needs to return to the bush. But a baby wombat who has been brought up by people will always die if it is just let loose in the bush. They have to learn how to find wombat burrows, shelter from heat and daylight, and find food and water. So they need a halfway house where they can live for a few months or a year — a house in the bush where there are caring people who will look after them — and where the wombat can find out that wombats don't always sleep on sofas and that the best wombat food doesn't come from cupboards.

Sometimes the wombat only stays with its new carers for a few weeks and then wanders off into the bush; other times it may stay for years. Mostly they stay until they are about eighteen months old, slowly padding off for longer and longer trips away from home, until one day we realise it has been months since we saw them — and we may never see them again.

An angry wombat

Wombats may seem to forget you when they leave home. But sometimes something will make them remember you again. Mothball left home when she was eighteen months old. A year later she was back again — and angry.

The world was hot and dry and she blamed us. No matter how many bowls of oats, wombat nuts or carrots I put down, Mothball wanted revenge — and she attacked anything that smelled of humans!

She bashed up the garbage bin. She chewed up the garden chairs. She dragged a box over so she could climb up and rip the mop to shreds.

She wrecked the flower pots. She ate the garden table. She ripped the clothes from the clothes line, so finally we had to take our washing up to town, where it would be safe from wombat teeth.

She attacked the spade, Bryan's boots, and a shopping bag I put down for ten seconds. I waited for a *clang* every night which might mean she'd decided to eat the car.

When she began to gnaw the window frame Bryan raced into town and bought reinforcing mesh and nailed it around the house. Our place looks like it has been barricaded against an army of angry gnomes. But it's just protected against one small, angry wombat.

And then it rained. And rained. And Mothball started eating grass. And eating. And eating, with the steady sweep of any animal who has been through a drought.

And she totally forgot about us until the next
time the drought bit hard, and there was an
angry wombat at the back door again yelling
'Gnaaa' which means, 'Feed me now if you
value your back door!'

Looking after a baby wombat

If you see a dead wombat by the side of the road, stop
and see if it has a baby in its pouch. (It will be pretty
obvious if the wombat is a male when you turn it over.)

If the baby is standing by its mother, try to catch it
even if it runs into the bush — a baby at this age
probably won't last long on its own and a few months
of care will give it a much better chance of survival.

Remember that the baby will be terrified, in a
strange world with noise and people. Don't try to
comfort the baby as you would a dog, by speaking to
it and patting it. Keep it in a dark, quiet place if you
can.

Don't try to care for the baby wombat yourself.
First of all it's *illegal* — and for very good reasons.
Too many people have tried to rear a young wombat
on condensed milk, soy milk, bread and marmalade,
and so on, treating it like a dog or a human baby. The
baby wombat may survive, but it won't become a
healthy adult. You have just had fun with a baby
animal, but not really helped the wombat.

But if you love wombats, *do* join one of the wildlife carers' associations, where you will be properly trained to care for orphans. You, too, can then have your life totally disrupted by a small, furry dictator who will insist that you play with it all night long and nurse it all day while it sleeps, eats every couple of hours, leaves droppings in your kitchen cupboards, rips up your bedspread, tunnels through your dirty clothes basket, destroys the garden — and creates other forms of wombat mayhem to keep your life interesting.

In return you will have months with possibly the universe's most cuddly and infuriating creature. You'll also have the heartbreak of saying goodbye to them when they go bush again. But it's a joyous kind of heartbreak, as you will know that the wombat is leaving for a life of real fulfilment that it can no longer get with its human carers.

Please, never keep a wombat for more than eighteen months. The wombat may seem happy with you, but it's like the happiness a human would feel being kept as a pet by aliens and living in a comfortable room, fed slops and petted by alien children! The human might seem content, but that would be because their prison was all they knew.

It is not fair to turn a wombat into a long-term pet. Wombats are wild animals. They need to be free.

Tips on caring for a baby wombat

First of all wrap the baby in something soft, like an old sheet, and keep it warm with a hot-water bottle or cuddle it next to you — the wombat's preferred heat is about the same as human body temperature, 36°C.

Keep the baby in as quiet and dark a place as possible — a pouch made from an old sack or a pillow case, well padded and slung over your shoulder during the day is great; at night you'll need to use a hot-water bottle and to replace it a couple of times during the night.

If you know it will take you more than a couple of hours to get the baby to qualified care (such as the Wildlife Information and Rescue Service — WIRES — which operates Australia-wide, or another wildlife rescue organisation) and if it's a hot day and you feel the baby has been without milk for more than a day, stop at the nearest vet clinic and ask for a marsupial teat and bottle to feed the baby sterilised water. Or buy a low lactose milk (like Divetalac) from the chemist. A baby wombat's mouth is very small and tender and can be damaged by a large human-size teat or by forcing a teaspoon of water or milk into its mouth.

The vet may know a wildlife carer, too, who may look after the baby. The vet may also be able to check if the baby is hurt. This isn't easy, though. I once took an injured wombat to a vet. But though the vet

checked her thoroughly he couldn't find where she'd been hurt. Wombats have a very high pain threshold. They don't even notice injuries that would have humans screaming in pain. This wombat had a cracked thigh bone, but she just thought that the vet was playing with her and giving her a cuddle. It's hard to work out what bit is hurt if your patient doesn't yell or flinch when it's touched!

Make sure you take the wombat to an agency like WIRES as soon as you can, where experts can care for it. If this is not an option, apply to your local national parks organisation or the equivalent for a licence to keep the baby, and ask WIRES or the national parks service for the most up-to-date information on keeping orphaned animals. (Be aware, though, that these recommendations are being reviewed fairly constantly, so what information you 'knew' for certain a few or many years ago may now be lamentably out of date. Make sure you are operating from the most recent recommendations based on the most current research.)

These are a few absolute essentials you need to know before caring for a baby wombat, even for a short time.

1. Milk requirements

Baby wombats need between 10% and 15% of their body weight in milk every day. You will need to weigh the wombat if you are not sure that it is getting enough milk and to check that it is putting on weight, just like you would with a human baby. For example, an 850-gram wombat will need at least 85 millilitres of milk a day, and probably more if the weather is hot and the baby is active (say about 130 millilitres a day).

This *must* be low lactose milk. You can now buy milk especially formulated for marsupials from Wambaroo Food Products in South Australia. Most vets in country areas now stock these. Other low lactose milk products may be used for a short time. Never feed a wombat cow's milk in any form at all, including condensed milk, or any vitamins or anything with sugar or salt in it.

2. Feeding requirements

Baby wombats need to be fed every two hours until their fur grows, and about every three hours after that right through the night too. Wombats are nocturnal, and you may find that your orphan goes to sleep on you during the day and just coaxing it to drink enough milk may take up a lot of your time. Normally a baby feeds almost constantly in its mother's pouch — and some wombats just don't ever fit in with the 'guzzle it fast then go back to sleep' pattern that baby humans follow. You will almost certainly have to keep waking up the baby to feed it; pulling the teat gently from its mouth is a good method — you want to wake it enough to feed, but not enough to make it want to wrestle you.

Most baby wombats prefer to feed lying on their back, which is the way wombats feed in the pouch, but I have known one wombat that demanded to be on her stomach. Try the back position first but don't try arguing with a wombat.

Never force-feed a wombat — you may force milk into its lungs and kill it. Just keep cuddling it and offering it the milk until it finds the smell and taste familiar enough to try a little.

If the wombat wants to be fed, feed it.

If the baby develops diarrhoea, dilute the milk with 50% sterilised water and get vet advice *immediately*.

Sterilise the teat and container after every feed and clean around the baby's mouth with a damp cloth to make sure there is no dried milk caking the baby's lips or chin. Change the bedding when it is soiled. There is a delicate balance here between hygiene — like any premature baby, an orphaned wombat is very susceptible to infections — and keeping a nice familiar wombat smell to reassure the baby.

After the baby has had its bottle, wipe the baby's anus as this may stimulate the wombat to urinate or defecate.

3. *General care*

If the baby doesn't have fur, wipe its body every day with lanolin and make sure its bedding is very soft.

When the baby is fully furred, though still pink rather than brown — about eight months old — let it

play on fresh, clean, short grass, green if possible. The baby should start to eat grass about now.

Don't let the baby feed on dry grass with hard stems or hay — they can puncture the intestine and the baby will die. If possible, give the baby access to other wombat droppings that will provide useful bacteria for its stomach; and don't worry if the baby eats its own scats. A baby wombat may also eat rolled oats, carrots or chunks of sweet potato or sweet corn, but these should just be a treat, not its main diet.

Your baby wombat will probably decide that it would like to try the cat's food, the dog's food, your toast, any cake on the coffee table and your socks. Remove all temptations — wombats will get diarrhoea from too much carbohydrate and they may get kidney damage from eating any other foods. Their food should be mostly milk and grass.

4. Play and discovery

Give the baby dirt to play and dig in and branches to gnaw, and make sure it gets lots of walks on grass and through bushland as much as possible, so it learns about space and scents and terrain — the baby won't run away from you and get lost. On the contrary, baby wombat's will keep you carefully within bumping distance! They are only really happy if they can touch your ankle with their nose!

Don't worry if their claws are long — they need to be long to dig, so don't file them off or think that, like dogs, they need to run on concrete or hard ground to wear them down.

Play with baby wombats as much as possible — lots of rough and tumble and tugs of war to develop their muscles and coordination. Let the baby follow you around the garden or anywhere that is safe from dogs and cars. In fact don't let the wombat spend much time around dogs and cars — it may run towards both in later life, hoping to find you, and be killed.

Don't let the baby out in the hot sun too much — it can die of heat prostration or get a dry skin that may get infected.

Don't punish a wombat. You can't train a wombat, but you can scare it. A hurt wombat will learn to fear you, but it won't learn to be toilet-trained or to ignore the cat food or not to dig through the dining room floor, or through your bedroom door if it is lonely.

The joy and despair of living with a wombat is accommodating yourself to a wombat's desires!

The only way I know to encourage a wombat to use a toilet spot is to find a nice dark cupboard or wardrobe — the broom cupboard is great, as brooms have such interesting smells — line it with lots of newspaper and put some of its droppings there, to encourage it to keep using that area. Or if it chooses another place, go with the flow and line it with paper so the droppings are at least manageable.

5. *Back into the wild*

When the wombat is about ten months old you should begin finding it a halfway house where it can come and go at will but still be bottle fed — the wombat will gradually learn how to cope with the bush and other animals.

Don't worry that your baby wombat will wander away and not be able to find its way back. Wombats are even better than dogs at smelling their way back.

When a wombat is about a year old it should be living in a burrow within a fenced area to keep it safe from dogs and other dangers, as it roams at night. (If you have a secure 'orphan burrow' the baby may choose to live in it much earlier, but don't force it if it is scared.)

By the time the wombat is eighteen months old make sure it can wander back to the bush and freedom, so it can wander off freely without a farewell grunt to you. You'll probably cry a bit. But there will be memories and, while our bush survives, more wombats to take its place. And if you're lucky you will probably see it again, living a wombat life in the distance.

Mange and ticks

Most wombats get mange at some time. Mange is a tiny mite — *Sarcoptes scabei* — that burrows into the skin to lay its eggs. The itch is agonising. Wombats will scratch so hard they tear their skin, and those scratches can become infected or maggot-ridden. Great mange crusts form all over the wombat's body. Their eyes may be so crusty they can't see and their ears may be so misshapen they can't hear either.

Mange is spread from wombat to wombat, usually in an infected wombat burrow; it is also spread by dogs, dingoes and foxes.

Around our area mange is worst in hot dry seasons. Hunger drives wombats out in the sunlight and the dry air and heat irritates the wombat's skin and they catch mange more easily. A hungry or sick wombat also seems to get mange more often. (See Chapter 12 for how mange can be treated.)

Wombats are also attacked by wombat ticks that suck their blood, as well as a few other ticks (they usually don't get the paralysis or 'dog' tick, though). Mostly wombats don't seem bothered by these ticks except when they are poorly fed or stressed in other ways. At these times the added burden of ticks can kill them.

Gabby — a sad wombat story

I learned about the downside of looking after baby wombats when I met Gabby. All the other wombats we had cared for happily went bush. But Gabby was different.

Gabby was the dumbest wombat I have ever met. But she was the sweetest, too. Like Fudge, she came to us so we could teach her how to return to the bush.

I first realised Gabby was a bit intellectually challenged when I saw the cardboard box wandering around by itself in the grass beside the shed.

It wasn't moving very fast. I watched it for a while, then lifted it up.

There was a small wombat underneath. 'Gna, gna, gna?' Gabby enquired. She blinked, as though wondering why the sun had come out.

I lifted Gabby up and took her indoors. It was midday and even ten minutes of the heat might kill her.

Gabby's mother had been shot. Some bushwalkers had found baby Gabby and took her back to Canberra and gave her to WIRES. Gabby was nearly dead from heat and thirst — and probably terror, too. But she survived.

Gabby was brought up with two other orphaned wombats, a few months older than she was. She was always a quiet wombat and just liked to be cuddled and to pad after the other two orphans while they raced around the garden.

Gabby was still too young to go with her two foster brothers when they returned to the bush. But Gabby missed the other wombats. She wouldn't eat. Worse, she began to scratch, so badly that she tore her skin.

Her carers took her to a vet, who said she must have mange, and gave her an injection.

But Gabby was still depressed.

So Gabby's carers gave her to us. There was fresh grass and good smells to tempt her in our valley.

But Gabby didn't want to be a wombat. If I pushed her into the wombat hole behind the bathroom when she was almost asleep she'd stay there until she woke up again. But she never went in the hole by herself.

Gabby chased cars, because cars meant humans and Gabby loved humans. We put up 'Beware: wombat' signs on the road on our farm. Gabby thought the best life in the world was sitting on a sofa with a human stroking her.

One month went by, then two. Gabby no longer wanted her bottle, but she wouldn't eat either — not even wombat nuts, a mix of grain and compressed lucerne made specially for native animals. The only way I could get her to eat anything was to cradle her, and let her eat out of my hand. But it took an hour just to get her to eat half a dozen mouthfuls. And she got thinner and thinner.

I called WIRES, the vet, every wombat person I could think of. I tried tempting her with celery root or raw sweet corn. I tried soaking oats or wombat nuts in Wombaroo, the special milk formulated for baby marsupials. But she still ignored them.

Then a friend brought down her guide dog, Katy, for the day. Normally we don't allow dogs here — some native animals will die of thirst rather than cross the scent trail of a dog to get to the creek and, besides, I didn't want the wombats to get used to the scent of dogs.

Elaine put down a dish of dried dog food for Katy while I cooked dinner for the rest of us.

There was a noise behind me. Gabby had climbed down from the sofa. She trotted across the floor to the dog food.

Katy was a dog in a million. She stepped politely away from her dinner as Gabby crunched at the dog food.

Dry dog food is *not* good food for wombats. But Gabby loved it — and was obviously familiar with it. Had her carers fed her dog food? Or had there been a dog in the house and Gabby had shared its meals?

Finally Gabby stopped and waddled back to the sofa. As far as she was concerned, she'd had her first decent meal since she arrived.

I rang the vet, who told me what I'd assumed: dog biscuits were far too salty and high in protein for wombats. But he said a few wouldn't hurt — especially as she wouldn't eat anything else.

I decided to give her dog biscuits only in the mornings, after a night's grazing. If she was hungry at night she'd eat grass, I reasoned, then she could have a few biscuits in the morning.

But Gabby wouldn't graze at night. She slept when we did. Gabby was too humanised — and too brain damaged too, I suspect — ever to be a wild wombat. And she hated to be alone. I left her sleeping one morning while I went to plant more beans and cauliflowers. I heard a noise outside the garden.

'Gna, gna, gna?' Gabby had followed my trail out to the garden.

'I'm here,' I yelled.

'Gna, gna, gna?' Gabby tried to work out where the sound came from, then sniffed instead and headed my way. Wombats don't need to put their nose to the ground to follow a trail, as dogs do. A scent to them is like a bit of rope from their nose that leads to the object they are after.

Bump. Gabby had come up against the reinforcing mesh that guarded our lettuce and carrots and cauliflowers from the wallabies.

Another wombat would have kept on pushing or tried to bite through it or begun a tunnel. Gabby was too sweet and timid for that.

'Gna, gna, gna?' she asked hopefully.

Cling. Cling. Clang.

I stared.

Gabby was climbing up the reinforcing mesh.

I know it is impossible. Wombats can't climb. There is absolutely no way they can climb. But Gabby was, rung by rung by rung, until she reached the top. She balanced there for about two seconds. Then she fell forwards.

Whump. She hit the ground head first.

'Gna, gna, gna?'

I raced over to her and carried her out of the garden. And after that I made sure I left the gate open for her.

Gabby was fifteen months old now, but she was no larger than a ten-month-old wombat. And she was still terribly thin.

Winter passed, and then spring. Gabby had stopped growing. And as the weather grew hotter she almost stopped eating too. She refused to eat grass at all now, or carrots or lettuce or anything we tempted her with.

Gabby's only talent was tracking. One day she heard splashing and laughter down at the swimming hole and wanted to join in the fun.

'Gna, gna, gna?' Gabby padded down the track to the swimming hole, found the exact spot I'd gone into the water and ...

'Gna, gna, gna?'

'Stop, you dingbat wombat!' I yelled.

But Gabby kept on going. She didn't even notice the water. She didn't notice when her head went under either. She just kept padding forward as the water rose above her head. My son dived down and hauled her up. She didn't struggle. She just hung limply in his arms, snorting and choking.

I took Gabby from him and waded to the bank and sat down with her on my lap. Her breathing was normal again now. Within seconds she was asleep. Had she just stopped breathing when she hit the water? I still have no idea how she survived.

I carried her back to the house. From now on one of us would have to babysit the wombat.

You can't really imprison a wombat, not unless they accept their prison. Locking Gabby in the bathroom while we had a swim was no use. By the time we'd made it to the front gate she would have torn the towels to shreds, unrolled the toilet paper and tried to burrow through the bath.

Besides, it was cruel. Gabby had simply never learned to be a self-sufficient adult. She was still a baby, even though she was two years old.

The summer grew hotter. It was impossible to be with Gabby constantly, although I did my best. And now she had mange again.

I wasn't surprised. Mange is a constant problem with wombats where we live, and even though we manage to treat most of the wombats near the house there are always strange ones visiting and bringing the infection.

The vet gave me medicine for her. I waited until she was asleep on my lap, then injected her quickly. She hardly twitched the first time, or even the next time the injection was due.

But she kept on scratching.

We injected her twice more, but the scratching continued. Her droppings were loose now, too, a side effect of the drugs.

I took her to the vet and he gave her yet another injection, and a soothing cream to rub on. Gabby's diarrhoea got worse. And she still scratched.

At last I tried an old remedy — powdered sulphur, mixed with Sorbolene. It is not easy to rub Sorbolene and sulphur onto a struggling wombat. But Gabby just thought it was a game, a nice wriggly game where in the end I, too, was coated in the bright yellow mixture.

Gabby stopped scratching. But as the weather grew hotter she had even less appetite and her bowels still hadn't recovered. The vet could do nothing to help her. And she was still so very small.

I spent a large part of each day cuddling her. The rest of the day she spent in my study, nosing around the bookshelves and sleeping on a cushion or a pile of magazines or the page proofs for the next book. I'd given up all attempts to get her to go wild.

Finally, early one morning, when I took her out to try to tempt her with some grass, she padded over to the wombat burrow behind the bathroom and climbed inside.

It was the first time she had gone in there by herself. I grinned and went inside for breakfast. Maybe Gabby was just a slow learner. Maybe in a few months she'd be eating grass and living in the burrow …

She hadn't come out again by morning-tea time. I thought she must have decided to sleep there all day. But there was no sign of Gabby at dinner time, either.

By now I was worried. I sat at the entrance to the burrow and called her, banging on the rock by the entrance over and over to attract her attention.

Still no sign of Gabby.

I tried to tell myself that she was exhausted. She'd come out late at night and begin to chomp the grass.

Midnight, and still no sign of Gabby.

It was hard to sleep. I kept listening for the sounds of chomping, or a *gna, gna, gna* or a whimper in the night.

Morning. No wombat prints outside the bathroom.

The burrow was too small for me to get into. I shone a torch in as far as I could, and called again.

There was no sound. No movement.

So we waited. There was nothing else to do. And three days later there was a smell of death from the wombat burrow — and there was no use hoping any more.

I failed Gabby, though I still don't know what more I could have done. I shall always feel ashamed that she chose to die alone, not in my lap. But I know I am wrong to feel that. Gabby's last moments were spent as a wombat likes to live, in the cool dark peace of her burrow.

12

Living with Wombats Around You

Though wombats are wild animals, they often decide to live around humans, especially if humans have plonked themselves and their new house in wombat territory. They also like humans' neatly mown and watered green lawns and the nice bare dirt under their houses to dig in!

How to live with a wombat

If you want to live with a wombat there are various things you should do.

1. Make your house wombat-friendly.

If a wombat decides to live under your house and you are worried about its foundations — or just don't like being woken up at two o'clock in the morning by a scratching or digging wombat — net around the foundations so wombats can't get in. You will need to bury the netting half a metre deep, too, or the wombat will dig underneath it.

If the wombat is under your house and you can't get it out, put in a one-way wombat flap that can be pushed out but not in. This way when the wombat goes out to graze it won't be able to get in again.

But do check the next day to make sure the wombat isn't stranded in daylight. It will probably have another burrow to shelter in but — particularly in droughts or if you have recently ploughed the paddocks around or put in cattle — their burrow may have been destroyed and heat and sunlight can kill a wombat.

2. Don't have a dog.

If you already have a dog, train it to avoid the wombat and keep it indoors at night. Make sure visitors with dogs keep them on leashes or indoors, especially at night.

3. Don't pat the wombat!

I never try to touch wild wombats, and only feed the ones that have learned to share Mothball's meals, and then only in a bad drought. Wombats need to know that people — and their dogs and cars — are dangerous.

Most authorities say *never* feed a wild animal. Even in bad times a wombat should find most of its own food, not get it from you. Droughts are a natural way of making sure that only strong wombats survive.

Never feed wild animals or birds so much that they become dependent on you — or stay around when they need to go away for winter or in a drought. But a little food can greatly increase a wombat's quality of life when things are tough and can make them strong enough to go further in search of their own food (and a little watering of the grass may do more good than putting out wombat nuts or oats).

Do make sure you feed wombats the right sort of food (see Chapter 11). But a wild wombat is unlikely to eat anything you put down for it, unless another wombat teaches it that this is good food.

4. Protect your fences with wombat gates.
No fence stops a wombat. If they can't push through it they'll dig underneath. If you've spent days putting in a fence to keep rabbits or lambs out, it will take a wombat only a few minutes to undo all your good work!

The answer to this is wombat gates. Wombats will keep using the same tunnel under the fence — and will push through anything blocking their way to it rather than try to dig a new one. They are also so strong they can push through a gate that is too heavy for lambs, rabbits or wallabies.

You can swing a neatly-made gate made out of wood and wire across the hole the wombat made in the fence — or try an old car tyre filled with old fencing wire.

Tie the tyre to the top of the hole. It'll block rabbits and lambs, but a strong wombat will be able to push through it easily.

Another wombat 'gate' design we tried was simply an old, two-metre-long culvert pipe (broken and therefore bought cheaply from the council). We pushed this through the hole the wombat had dug underneath the fence. Wombats went down it happily but lambs and wallabies didn't like to crawl that far.

Bryan also ties a flap of two thicknesses of netting wire between two heavy bits of iron and ties this above the hole in the fence. The result: a heavy gate that wombats can push past, but wallabies can't.

Wombats can also be kept out with electric fences. Place two electrified wires on each side of the netting fence about 30 centimetres from the fence and 30 centimetres above the ground. This will also help to keep out wild dogs, dingoes and most foxes, and at least cut down the rabbit invasion.

5. *Find out about mange.*
If you have wombats around you'll always see a few with bad mange — and it's heartbreaking to watch them suffer. But luckily you can help them.

Mange can be treated, with a medicine given either in a wombat's food or by injection, or with a lotion

that is poured on their backs — as I've described in my story about Gabby, in the previous chapter. All of these have to be prescribed by a vet. Vets can also provide you with cream to soothe the irritation and help heal the crusty lesions.

It is difficult to get medicine into wombats' food unless you are feeding them regularly, and it can be hard to get close to some wombats. Wombats *really* dislike having the mange lotion poured on their backs, and once you've done it the first time they will keep well away from you when they smell it again!

Treating a wombat with mange

The easiest way to treat a wombat with mange is with a water pistol. Get the medicine and detailed instructions from the vet, and a pump action water pistol from a newsagent or toy shop. When you've worked out what the correct dose is for your wombat, practise a few times with water.

How do you get the right dose? You will need to know the approximate weight of the wombat to get the right dose of medicine either to feed it or to spray it with your water pistol.

As a rough guide, a fully grown, large wombat weighs between 30 and 45 kilograms. (Note that 45 kilograms is a very large wombat indeed!) A fully grown small wombat weighs about 16–25 kilograms.

An emaciated wombat weighs about 20 kilograms.

A young but independent wombat weighs about 15–25 kilograms. You can usually tell a young wombat from an old one by its bum — a young wombat has a more pointed bum, while a mature wombat's bum is rounded. But an emaciated old wombat will also have a more pointed bum. The face of a young wombat may look more pointed and its ears bigger in proportion to its head, but wombats vary in face shape.

(If the wombat is hand-reared, though, you can weigh it. Cradle the wombat and stand on the scales. Then put the wombat down and weigh yourself. Subtract your weight from the other weight to find the weight of the wombat.)

Now, jet the wombat with the water pistol! Aim at the wombat's back or its side — not its head and certainly not near its eyes. You will need to repeat this, and perhaps treat the burrow too. Your vet will tell you how often it needs to be done.

Even once you have killed the mange parasite, the wombat may continue to scratch — and these scratches may get infected or become fly-blown. Wombats will roll in dust or mud to cover injury sites and keep flies off and do seem very resistant to infection. They live with the most grotesque wounds and even recover without human help.

Tame wombats can be rubbed with soothing creams

— again, ask your vet. But don't try this with wild wombats unless you are a very experienced wombat handler, as you might get badly hurt and so might the wombat.

You should be aware that not all vets are familiar with wombats or how to treat mange, so you may need to seek out one who is (or who will find out how to help you). WIRES and other wildlife organisations also have lists of vets who specialise in native animals.

13

Protecting Wombats

Wombats are not endangered, but in many areas they are disappearing. If there are too few wombats in an area there won't be enough adults to breed another healthy generation of wombats.

What kills wombats?
Wombats numbers are declining for various reasons.

1. Cars
Wombats like eating along the edge of the road because cattle and sheep usually don't graze there, so there is a lot of green grass — and the moisture from dew or any rain that falls on the road washes onto the side too, so even in dry periods there's often a bit of green grass by the road.

Wombats will never learn to be careful of cars

because they can't smell a car approaching — by the time they smell it the car is on them.

2. *Too many cattle, horses or sheep in a paddock*
Cattle, sheep and horses eat the wombat's food, and their heavy feet can flatten wombat burrows.

3. *Land fenced off for gardens or farming*
Even if you don't eat meat — or keep horses or other livestock — the food that has been grown for you to eat still takes away the place where a wombat might graze. People can grow fruit and vegetables and still coexist with wombats but most farming methods aren't friendly to wombats and other wild animals. At our farm we work out ways to grow fruit and vegetables *and* welcome wild animals like wombats and wallabies. (See my website for more details.)

Do paddocks have too many wombats?

Often farmers think they have lots of wombats eating their grass, but there may be only one or two. If you wonder how many wombats you're supporting, count the *fresh* scats — the soft, moist ones — then divide by a hundred, as we know that one wombat produces about a hundred scats a night.

Wombats are also blamed for fouling dams. Wombats don't foul dams — and may not even drink if pasture is lush.

4. Fire

When there is a fire wombats suffocate down in their burrows and burnt ground is more likely to collapse. Wombats starve if all their grass has been burnt.

No wombat can dig fast enough to escape a fire.

Wombats die in bushfires, but they are also killed in control burns — when the bush is burned to help prevent a larger fire. Often these fires aren't controlled at all and are even more savage than a bushfire. Control fires should be lit only in cool weather and when there is no wind, and by people who know what they are doing.

5. Illegal activities

Wombats frequently die from poisoned grain and baits meant for rabbits and birds. They are also maimed or killed in wild dog traps. Many wombats are shot by farmers because they make holes in fences or because the farmers feel that a wild animal has no place on their farm.

It is against the law to kill native animals. If you know of anyone who kills, traps or poisons wombats call the police, the RSPCA or the national parks organisation in your state. They may not do anything, even if you can prove it. But if enough people start making a fuss when wild animals are killed illegally the authorities will have to start taking action.

What can you do?

You can do various things to help wombats.

- Ask your council and local farmers to keep the edge of roads ploughed, so wombats don't graze there and get run over.
- Ask your council to put wildlife tunnels under roads so animals can cross safely — a wombat will follow the scent of other wombats and use a tunnel if it's there. Wombat tunnels don't have to be very big — a stormwater pipe makes a great wombat crossing!
- Ask farmers to leave some bush for wildlife and to connect bits of bush up so animals can move between them. In dry times wombats and other wild animals need water and grass — cattle can be moved to a wetter area in a drought, but wombats have to stay with their patch of territory. Maybe city people should pay farmers to keep some of their land for wombats instead of using it all to make a living.
- Write to your Member of Parliament asking that police and national parks rangers really *do* act when wombats are illegally shot or trapped.
- Write to your Member of Parliament asking for more national parks — and for more money to be allocated to keep wild goats and other feral pests out of national parks, so there is food for wildlife, and more money to train more national parks and

forestry workers on how to manage fire properly, so it doesn't flare out of control.

🐝 Pay 'rent' to wildlife. Wild animals and birds were here before we were, so we should make sure we let them have some of the grass, the water, the fruit — and maybe a few carrots if they want them!

As human beings we evolved with lots of other animals around us and with trees and flowers and other living things. I know that when I'm in cities, surrounded by only people and their products, I find life very simple. Life is much richer when there are wild animals living their own lives around you.

I share my land with wild animals, mostly for myself, because without other species I would be less.

14

Writing with Wombats as My Muse

A wombat got my first book published. The wombat's name was Smudge. The shed where I lived in those days was in the middle of his territory. Every evening he'd come in and look around the shed … and if I didn't leave the door open for him he'd knock it down.

I was broke. I needed $106.44 to register my car. But there was a drought, so there was no water to grow vegetables or fruit trees, and I had a baby to look after, too. And then I thought, *maybe* I can write a book.

Smudge and the typewriter

I had been writing stories all my life, just scribbling them on scraps of paper, but had never had the courage to send one to a publisher. Now I was desperate.

But I couldn't send a scribbled bit of paper to a publisher. I'd had an old typewriter when I was at university, but that had broken down years before, and there was no way I could afford to buy a new one now.

In those days I never went to the dump to leave rubbish — all my 'rubbish' was fed to the chooks or turned into compost. But I did call in at the dump whenever I went to town to see if someone had left something useful — old fruit boxes or chairs that could be repaired or old tanks that I could patch with cement and use for storing water for the garden or keeping firewood dry.

And one morning there was a typewriter, sitting in the middle of the pile. I clambered over the dead sheep and some smelly dog food cans, hauled the machine back home and tried it. It still worked!

I didn't have a desk. But I did have an old door — it's the door to my bathroom now. So I propped the door up on stacks of bricks and put the typewriter on it and sat down cross-legged on the floor and began to write my stories.

Most of them were pretty bad — it had been years since I'd really worked at what I wrote. But I was extraordinarily happy to be writing again.

But Smudge hated that typewriter. I think it was the noise he hated — the *tappa, tappa, bing!* of an old-fashioned typewriter. Every night, after I'd gone to bed, I'd hear him nose his way around the shed, sniffing at the typewriter — and every morning there'd be a large wombat dropping on it, just to make it clear that this was *his* territory, typewriter and all.

Every morning I'd clean off the wombat dropping and start work again. But after three months of wombat droppings on the typewriter, my 'new' typewriter didn't work very well. In fact the 'e' wouldn't work at all — it was all soft and squishy when I pressed it. But all the other letters worked.

So I kept writing. Then one night, sitting on a rock in the dry creek bed, looking at Smudge nose about for shreds of grass, I remembered the rainstones I'd seen when I was working in a museum in Queensland. They were in a tobacco tin, with the label 'On no account ever open to the air'.

And suddenly the story came to me: about a girl who hopes the drought might break if she can find an Aboriginal who will use his rainstones. But the only Aboriginal guy around is the local building inspector, who grew up in Redfern, not the bush.

I trotted back to the shed and wrote *Rainstones*, while Smudge chomped outside the shed then dozed on the doorstep, twitching his nose in annoyance whenever my typewriter went *bing*!

I finished the story that night. And then I filled in all the 'e's that were missing.

It looked pretty messy — okay, *very* messy — the paper all old and yellow at the edges, with a few wombat dropping smudges, and all the 'e's done by hand. My spelling was terrible, too — I'm dyslexic and have never been able to spell well. But maybe, I thought hopefully, my spelling had improved since I'd left university.

I had no idea how to get a book published, but I thought there were probably publishers in Sydney. I drove the old green truck to town and called in at the post office, and looked up publishers in the Sydney telephone directory. The first publisher was Angus and Robertson, because they began with 'a'. So I sent it to them.

I heard years later what happened. The editor who pulled my story out of the envelope yelled, 'Hey, look at this mess, everyone! Look what someone has sent in!'

She said it was the worst spelled, messiest manuscript anyone had ever submitted. And because it was so messy — and the spelling so bad — she thought it would be unintentionally hilarious. So she sat down to read a bit aloud to everyone so they could laugh at it.

She read one paragraph. She read another paragraph, then she read the whole story aloud — and three weeks later they sent me a cheque to publish it.

Suddenly I was a writer. And I owed it all to Smudge.

Mothball and *Diary of a Wombat*

More books followed — and more wombats. And then I met Mothball, and life has never been quite the same since.

She was a sweet-looking little wombat. Mothball had been through a lot. She was found in Canberra, badly mauled by dogs, bleeding, terrified, only just alive. Her rescuers raced her to a vet who worked on her for hours, sewing up the gashes.

Mothball was a stubborn little thing. Despite her injuries, she recovered. But she was badly scarred and her fur came back in patches, as though she was moth-eaten. So they called her Mothball — a round little wombat in a coat of grey and white and brown.

'We'll miss her terribly,' said her carer. 'But at least we know she'll be going somewhere good.'

They gave me her blanket, with its rich familiar wombat smells, and a couple of carrots to keep her happy. We put her in the animal carry cage in my car. I drove off to the sound of crunching on the back seat.

I'd just got to the outskirts of Canberra when the crunching stopped. Mothball had finished her carrots.

'Hunh, hunh, hunh, hunh, hunh,' said a voice from the back seat.

I ignored her.

'Hunh, hunh, hunh, hunh, hunh!' said the voice more loudly.

I waited for her to go to sleep.

'Hunh, hunh, hunh, hunh, hunh!!!' The voice was angry now.

'Look,' I said, 'I don't have any more carrots! You'll have to wait until we get home.'

'Hunh, hunh, hunh, hunh, hunh!!!' The cage rocked back and forward, then tumbled onto the floor. I screeched the car to a stop on the edge of the highway. I peered into the back seat to check that Mothball was alright.

'Hunh, hunh, hunh, hunh, hunh!' Mothball was furious now!

'You'll have to be patient,' I told the wombat. She gave an indignant screech. Wombats are never patient.

I began to drive again. Ten kilometres, twenty.

'Grg, grg, grg.'

I glanced behind. Mothball was chewing the plastic bars of the cage.

I tried to calculate. If it takes one wombat ten minutes to chew through one bar of her cage, how long will it take a wombat to chew through six bars and climb out of the cage?

Sixty minutes. But it would take eighty minutes to get home. That left twenty minutes for a furious wombat to chew the car seats, the steering wheel, and me ...

I stopped in Bungendore and bought more carrots — *lots* of carrots. I shoved them all into the cage.

Crunch. Crunch. It was a happy sound, the sound of a wombat who is training her human to provide all the carrots she wants.

Mothball loved the wombat burrow behind the bathroom. She marched in, came out with dirt on her nose, raced back in again, then raced out to eat grass ... and more grass ... and more grass still.

Our grass was soft and green that year, and the creek sang down past the garden as it ran between its stones.

I watched Mothball for a while, then went inside.

'Hunh, hunh, hunh, hunh, hunh!' Something scratched at the back door. Mothball must have smelled my trail inside.

Surely she didn't want more carrots! Probably just needed a cuddle, I decided. I opened the door.

A small brown ball hurtled past me, into the bathroom, grabbed the toilet paper, trampled it, ripped the towels, shredded the bath mat, then raced out again — all in five seconds — and butted me on the ankle.

'Hunh, hunh, hunh, hunh, hunh!' Yes, please. Mothball did want more carrots.

I carried her down to the garden and pulled some carrots up, and washed them and gave them to her. Mothball crunched them happily. These were the freshest, crunchiest carrots she had ever eaten.

I made a note to buy carrots in town. We grow most of our own vegetables, but I had a feeling we didn't grow enough carrots for Mothball.

Mothball got fatter and fatter. She was almost totally circular by this time, with tiny legs and a wombat grin. Her fur had grown back to a rich deep brown.

Then she began to dig.

Mothball's first burrow was under the truck in the shed. That hole collapsed as soon as it was about twenty centimetres deep. But Mothball kept on trying, night after night. All that grass and carrot energy had to be used up somehow.

Then she began her second burrow. It was behind my study, in the herb garden. Mothball is a good digger. I went to bed one night with a herb garden and woke up the next morning with a metre-high pile of dirt.

It took Mothball three nights to finish her hole. Then I put the sprinkler on the garden.

Two minutes after that Mothball emerged, damp and disgusted. Her new burrow leaked! She marched back to the hole behind the bathroom.

Mothball decided to renovate the hole behind the

bathroom instead of digging a new one. Every morning Bryan carted a barrow load of dirt and rocks away.

Finally Mothball was ready to furnish her new home. As I tapped at my computer one day I watched Mothball pad back and forth between the garden and her hole, each time carrying a fresh branch of lavender to make her bed — it was the sweetest-smelling burrow around.

Then we decided to build a new bedroom, over the old herb garden, where Mothball had dug her first burrow. Ray, the builder, put down the last of the flooring as a round, brown wombat bum was disappearing into the burrow below.

Surely she wasn't moving back in?

But she was. Somehow Mothball guessed that now the wombat burrow had a wide, thick roof it would no longer fill up with water.

The trouble was, that was exactly where the stairs were going to be. We either had to move the house or move the wombat.

So we moved the house. Already I knew that there was no way on earth we could move Mothball!

Mothball now had the fanciest wombat burrow in Australia. It had a concrete path to its door, a flowerbed out the front, a giant back verandah and a nice front patio.

She also had us trained to feed her carrots on demand!

I was on the phone to a friend one day and every now and then I described what Mothball was doing.

'I can see her eating grass out the study window ...

' ... she's scratching now ...

'Now she's bashing at the back door for her carrots ...

' ... oops, she's attacking the doormat ...

'... oh dear, she's just chewed up Edward's jeans ... '

Suddenly the idea for *Diary of a Wombat* was born. I scribbled it down.

There weren't many words — most of the book would be pictures. I sent it to Lisa, my publisher, and she began the search for the perfect illustrator. Which wasn't easy.

You can buy pottery wombats in any gift shop now, or furry stuffed ones. But most look more like pigs or bears than wombats. This was a book about a real wombat — and the wombat in it had to be realistic too.

And then Bruce Whately returned to Australia after a number of years in the United States. We had known each other for years, but it took my publisher's genius to put our styles together.

It worked.

I opened up the parcel of Bruce's first rough sketches at our post box in town. They were so funny — and so perfect — that I laughed so much I had to lean against the car and passers-by wondered if I was okay.

It was exactly Mothball wombat — I had sent

Bruce a pile of photos — but it was so much more than that too. My story was about a brown wombat in a black night. Bruce had simplified the outlines, played around with shadings ... and suddenly there was magic.

We knew it would work even before the book came out. We just didn't know how well! *Diary of a Wombat* is a book that people *love*. And it is a shock, sometimes, to read it again and feel the magic work once more, familiar as it is.

How everything I know in life I owe to wombats

- Be determined.
- Enjoy every second of 'now' — the best grass, the best bed, the best wombat burrow.
- Be *very* determined.
- Never lose an opportunity to have a scratch or eat a carrot.
- Know your land, and love it.
- Pongs can be interesting too — and so can droppings!
- Think things through slowly before you make a move, then charge!

When a wombat 'sees' the land it can smell yesterday as well as today ... and maybe last year, too. Try to see the world like a wombat does. Know your land well enough to look at the past and try to see the future too.

When I make a decision these days I think: what would a wombat think of that? The world would be a much better place if all politicians thought: will this make the world a better or a worse place for wombats?

Wombat Jokes

Many thanks to all the wombat lovers who
have sent in these jokes.

*How do you know that wombats are smarter
than chooks?*
Because no-one has ever eaten Kentucky
Fried Wombat!

Why did the wombat cross the road?
It didn't. The grass was on *this* side.

Why did Mothball wombat cross the road?
To bite the chicken before it could get to her carrots.

*What do you get if you cross a gorilla
with a wombat?*
A *gigantic* wombat burrow!

Why did the mother wombat growl at her baby?
Because it tried to read in bed.

Why do wombats carry their baby in a pouch?
Because you can't fit a pram down a wombat burrow.

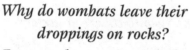

Why do wombats leave their droppings on rocks?
Because they can't reach the toilet.

What do you get if you cross a wombat with an owl?
A wombat who doesn't give a hoot.

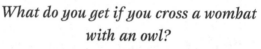

Why did the toilet paper roll down the wombat burrow?
Because it wanted to reach the bottom.
Why don't wombats fly north for the winter?
Because they don't serve grass on planes.

Why do mother wombats want their babies to sleep in a pouch?
Because then they don't keep them awake watching television.

What happens if you cross a wombat with
an elephant?
I don't know, but I hope it doesn't dig a burrow
under my house!

What happened when the mad scientist crossed a
vampire with a wombat?
It bit his neck then ate his carrots.

What happens if a wombat tries to dance with a cow?
It's udder chaos.

What's the hardest part about milking a wombat?
Getting a small enough bucket.

What's a wombat's favourite movie?
WomBatman.

What do you get if you cross a river with a wombat?
Wet.

What should you do if you find a wombat sitting on your seat at school?
Sit somewhere else.

What's brown and hairy and makes a lot of noise?
A wombat with a drum kit!

What comes out of a wombat's bum and sounds like a bell?
Dung!

Index